WOMEN
OF THE IRISH REVOLUTION

WOMEN
OF THE IRISH REVOLUTION

LIZ GILLIS

SUPPORTED BY

FOUNDED IN 1828
GLASNEVIN TRUST

DARDISTOWN   GLASNEVIN   GOLDENBRIDGE
NEWLANDS CROSS   PALMERSTOWN

MERCIER PRESS
IRISH PUBLISHER – IRISH STORY

This book is dedicated to Marie Gill, who like the women in this book was an inspiration. Through her sheer determination she gave so many people a future. She was a lady, a fighter and had such a revolutionary spirit. We miss you.

MERCIER PRESS
Cork
www.mercierpress.ie

© Liz Gillis, 2014

ISBN: 978 1 78117 205 6

10 9 8 7 6 5 4 3 2 1

A CIP record for this title is available from the British Library.

Printed and bound in the EU.

CONTENTS

ABBREVIATIONS

BMH	Bureau of Military History
GPO	General Post Office, Dublin
ICA	Irish Citizen Army
INAAVDF	Irish National Aid and Volunteer Dependants' Fund
IRA	Irish Republican Army
IRB	Irish Republican Brotherhood
ITGWU	Irish Transport and General Workers' Union
IWWU	Irish Women Workers' Union
NDU	North Dublin Union
O/C	Commanding officer
RIC	Royal Irish Constabulary
UVF	Ulster Volunteer Force

INTRODUCTION

Each time a girl opens a book and reads a womanless history, she learns she is worth less.

Myra Pollack Sadler

Important events throughout history all over the world are often seen to be men's history. The role that women have played in very important events is generally lost in the wider narrative and if one decides to look at or study women's roles in past events, more often than not the research is pigeonholed into the study of feminism. And while there is a need to look at the role of women in history from that perspective, it is a limited study. When historians look at certain events of the past where the main protagonists are men, there is no label, it is just history. This should also be the case when studying the role that women played in crucial events all over the world throughout the ages. This is certainly true of the part played by the women in Ireland between the years 1900–23, when Ireland won its independence, although not full independence, from Great Britain.

Ireland at the end of the nineteenth and in the early twentieth centuries was going through great change, especially where women were concerned. Women were becoming more political. Education, particularly a college degree, was becoming more accessible to both men and women, and not just those from a wealthy background. And it was through education that so many women realised they had a role to play in the future of their country. With organisations such as the Ladies' Land League, the Suffragettes and the Suffragists, women with similar attitudes and political opinions came together.

One of the most important women's organisations to be established was Inghinidhe na hÉireann, founded by Maud Gonne in Dublin in 1900. Although it was only to last fourteen years, this organisation was to have a strong influence on both the men and women who would go on to fight for Irish freedom. Inghinidhe was way ahead of its time, not just as a revolutionary movement advocating the cause of Irish freedom five years before Arthur Griffith founded Sinn Féin, but more importantly it was a social revolutionary movement. Its members saw the reality of everyday life for ordinary people, and particularly the poorer people in Dublin's inner city who had little chance of providing a better life for their families. These people experienced the highest rates of infant mortality in Europe and lived in what many would say were the worst slums in the whole of Europe. Inghinidhe sought to change this and set up schools for those children in the inner city denied an education. They believed that these children should at least be given a chance at a better life. They knew that education meant power and freedom, and they carried out their work with very little funding. It was to Inghinidhe that the Church turned for help in feeding the poorest children in society, a task which they carried out successfully and again on a very limited budget. It was this social awareness that set the women apart from the men over the coming years.

By 1912 the political climate in Ireland was changing. There was the promise from the British government that Home Rule for Ireland, which had long been the hope of so many nationalists, would become a reality. But Home Rule was not desired by all on the island and in 1913 the Ulster Volunteer Force (UVF) was founded to oppose the introduction of Home Rule, even if that meant their taking up arms against the British government. In November of that year the Irish Citizen Army (ICA) and the Irish Volunteers were also established. The ICA was set up to protect the labourers who were on strike in Dublin from the harassment of the police, while the Irish Volunteers were established to 'secure and maintain the rights and liberties common to the whole people of Ireland'.

With so much going on, it was believed that it was time for a new organisation for the women of Ireland, one that would build on what Inghinidhe had started but would hopefully become a nationwide organisation, unlike Inghinidhe, which only existed in Dublin. On 2 April 1914 Cumann na mBan was founded in Wynn's Hotel, Dublin. Inghinidhe na hÉireann was amalgamated into this new organisation, which sought to play its part in helping to achieve Irish independence. Some women felt that Cumann na mBan was actually limiting the contribution that women had to offer but, as events over the next ten years were to show, it was not a subservient body – these women would prove themselves above and beyond the call of duty in their dedication to the cause of Irish freedom.

During the Easter Rising the women of Cumann na mBan and the ICA stood beside their male counterparts. In the Marrowbone Lane Distillery, for example, there were twenty-three women who, upon the surrender of the garrison, were told to leave and save themselves. They refused. They had served with the men and they would share their fate. In all seventy-seven women were arrested and imprisoned after the Rising. The Easter Rising had not been supported by most Irish people – in its aftermath Dublin city lay in ruins, hundreds of civilians had been killed or wounded and the rebels were seen as disloyal to the thousands of Irishmen who were fighting in the British Army in the trenches in Europe – but public opinion began to change quickly with the executions of the leaders. Countess Markievicz was one of those sentenced to death for her involvement, serving as second in command to Michael Mallin at St Stephen's Green and the College of Surgeons. However, the British government realised that while society may accept the executions of men, that would not be the case if they executed a woman. Markievicz's sentence was commuted to life imprisonment.

In the end it did not matter. In their reaction to the Rising the British government were seen by the people to have acted too severely and in a matter of weeks public opinion changed dramatically from one of anger against the rebels to one of sympathy for their cause. And this change in opinion was certainly helped by the actions of the women left behind; the widows, daughters, sisters and mothers of those men who had fought and were executed, and those who were in prison in England and Wales. What these women did was to show the men as people; they became more than just faceless names. They were husbands, fathers and sons, who had a life to live but who were willing to give up that life for the freedom of their country. The women organised remembrance Masses, they collected funds for the relatives of the deceased and they travelled to England and visited the prisons, bringing home news of the way the rebels were being treated. This work was the training ground for what was to come and the women proved themselves more than capable in carrying out the tasks required of them. They were to prove themselves experts in the field of propaganda.

During the War of Independence that followed, the women were vital cogs in the revolutionary machine. This has been borne out in many of the testimonies of their male comrades in the IRA. The fact of the matter was that there were simply certain jobs that only the women could do. They were couriers and nurses and they had to be available at a moment's notice to help wanted men escape from military raids, often pretending to be their sweetheart and walking through the gauntlet of a military presence. They were intelligence agents, organisers, they collected money for the IRA arms fund and the Prisoners' Dependants' Fund, and they transported weapons and ammunition around the country, often carrying out their work at night, after curfew and alone. They were ambassadors on the lecture circuit in America, raising awareness and money for the Republican cause. Many were disowned by families who did not approve of their activities. And throughout this they looked after their households, they cared for their families and they often experienced first-hand the effect of the British military machine.

When the Civil War came the women were not unaffected by the tensions that followed the signing of the Anglo-Irish Treaty in December 1921. Like the other Republican organisations, Cumann na mBan split into pro- and anti-Treaty factions, but in the case of the women who took the anti-Treaty side, they were portrayed as being led by their emotions, with their behaviour considered by many to be irrational. The women on both sides suffered no less than their male counterparts during the conflict.

When I began researching this book I knew that women had played a central role in the struggle for Irish freedom. What I did not realise was just how vital they were to the revolutionary movement. One thing that became clear to me is that there was a difference between the men and the women. Whereas the men were fighting for the Republic, the women, while also fighting for that ideal, were additionally fighting for real change. They asked what exactly this Republic would mean for the ordinary people, for the poorer parts of society. Would they in fact benefit in any way or would their situation remain the same? The women realised that the 1916 Proclamation, a document that promised equal rights to all its citizens, that protected every child in the country, was a document to live up to and they sought to uphold the ideals it set out. They set up hospitals and helped raise and distribute money for those in need. They were revolutionaries in the true sense of the word.

But while there were many women who chose to take part in the revolution, there were also many who did not, but were affected by it anyway. As has been proven throughout the centuries all over the world, in conflict it is the women and children who end up suffering the most. The Irish revolution was no different. There were those whose husbands had to go on the run, leaving them to raise young families. These women often became both mother and father – they had to ensure their children were fed, often with very little money. Many lost their husbands in the conflict, while many suffered at the hands of the military through raids on their houses, day or night, destruction of their possessions and home, and, sadly, through physical violence. These women, the mothers, wives and daughters of the men who were fighting the war, sacrificed just as much as those who actively participated. For many of them the life they had expected to lead was dramatically changed by the events that took place in Ireland in the years 1916–23. And of course there were those who sheltered and fed those IRA men on the run, who carried messages for them, who were not affiliated to any organisation but just did what little they could. The Irish revolution affected these women as well and their contribution must also be recognised.

Unfortunately the years after the revolution did not bring the freedom these women had fought so hard for. The country had won its independence, but that freedom did not apply fully to the women who had given so much. This can be seen with the Conditions of Employment Bill introduced by Fianna Fáil in 1935, which limited the rights of women to work after they were married, and also the 1937 Constitution, Article 41, 2.1 and 2.2, which ensured that the woman's place was in the home. To quote:

2.1   In particular, the State recognises that by her life within the home, woman gives to the State a support without which the common good cannot be achieved.

2.2   The State shall, therefore, endeavour to ensure that mothers shall not be obliged by economic necessity to engage in labour to the neglect of their duties in the home.

For many women this was a step too far. They had proven their worth in the years 1900–23 and they continued to prove their worth when the revolution was over. As Lil Conlon stated in her book *Cumann na mBan and the Women of Ireland 1913–25*: 'Very often it has been said – "What did the Women do anyway?"' The answer to this question is simple. The women did an awful lot. They did not wait to be asked to contribute to the revolutionary movement. They did what they had to do when it had to be done. And this contribution was accepted by the men when it was realised that to succeed they needed the help and support of the women, yet when the revolution was over their contribution was forgotten by many.

It has been said many times that the IRA was the invisible army, but that title must surely be applied to the women of Ireland. They were the invisible army. They lost friends, husbands, sweethearts and children, and bore the weight of the revolution. And for these women their stories did not end in 1923 or 1936 or indeed 1937. Many settled into domestic life, rearing their families and watching their children go on to succeed, to build on what they had started. Others went on to achieve great things in medicine, in literature, in education and to further the rights of women in the workplace and the rights of all workers. But one thing really stands out over the course of the years and that is the social conscience of these women. They were involved in setting up organisations such as Gorta, and they did great work with the St Vincent de Paul Society, the Irish White Cross and the Irish Red Cross.

These women, who were once subjects of the Empire, became the matriarchs of Ireland. They were our mothers, grandmothers, aunts, grand-aunts, neighbours and revolutionaries. And we today, not just the women of Ireland, but the people of Ireland, need to remember just exactly what these women did.

To have a strong, independent woman in one's life, especially for the young girls and young women in our society, or indeed any society, is something to embrace and cherish. We have had in this country so many independent, feisty, strong women who decided to stand up and fight for what they believed in, and they are to be admired and, above all, they must be remembered. They suffered and sacrificed for their beliefs, in the hope that their actions would lead to a better future for the generations that would follow them. They proved that with enough passion and determination the impossible can become a reality. We are fortunate to have them as our foundation stone. And it is our role to ensure that that foundation stone is preserved. It is the least we can do.

AUTHOR'S NOTE

Although the book is divided chronologically, most of the women played a part throughout the period. I have, therefore, placed them in the sections where we know most about their activities, but provided their entire revolutionary histories. As is the nature of the sources we know more about some of these women than others. Thus you will find some of the better-known women appearing in more than one section.

Liz Gillis

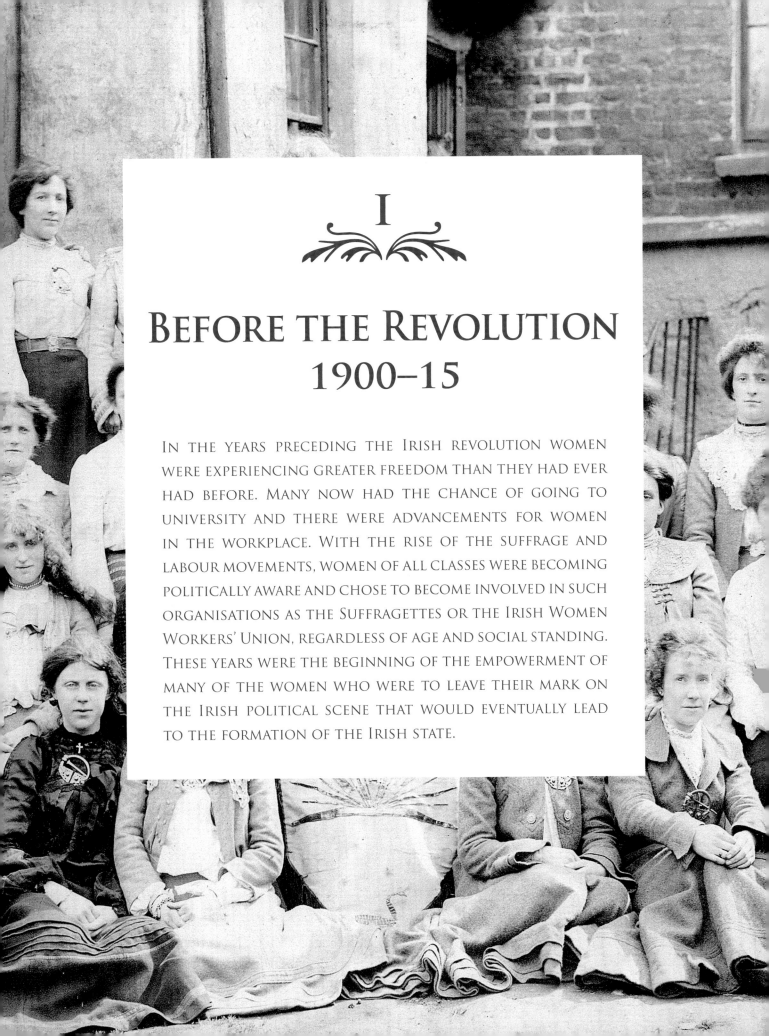

I

BEFORE THE REVOLUTION
1900–15

IN THE YEARS PRECEDING THE IRISH REVOLUTION WOMEN WERE EXPERIENCING GREATER FREEDOM THAN THEY HAD EVER HAD BEFORE. MANY NOW HAD THE CHANCE OF GOING TO UNIVERSITY AND THERE WERE ADVANCEMENTS FOR WOMEN IN THE WORKPLACE. WITH THE RISE OF THE SUFFRAGE AND LABOUR MOVEMENTS, WOMEN OF ALL CLASSES WERE BECOMING POLITICALLY AWARE AND CHOSE TO BECOME INVOLVED IN SUCH ORGANISATIONS AS THE SUFFRAGETTES OR THE IRISH WOMEN WORKERS' UNION, REGARDLESS OF AGE AND SOCIAL STANDING. THESE YEARS WERE THE BEGINNING OF THE EMPOWERMENT OF MANY OF THE WOMEN WHO WERE TO LEAVE THEIR MARK ON THE IRISH POLITICAL SCENE THAT WOULD EVENTUALLY LEAD TO THE FORMATION OF THE IRISH STATE.

Jennie Wyse Power (née O'Toole) was born in Baltinglass, Co. Wicklow, in 1858. In the 1880s she joined the Ladies' Land League and found herself immersed in their activities during the Land War, organising the League in Wicklow and Carlow. In 1883 she married John Wyse Power, a journalist who shared her political beliefs; he was a member of the Irish Republican Brotherhood (IRB). She was one of the first members of Inghinidhe na hÉireann upon its inception in 1900 and was elected as one of its four vice-presidents. In 1905 she became a member of Sinn Féin when it was founded by Arthur Griffith, and later became vice-president of the party. An advocate of women's suffrage, in 1904 she became a member of the committee of the Irish Women's Suffrage and Local Government Association, which had been set up by Anna and Thomas Haslam. She was also a member of the provisional committee that set up Cumann na mBan in 1914. Moreover, she was a successful business woman, having set up a grocery store and restaurant, the Irish Farm Produce Company, at 21 Henry Street. She later opened two more shops, in 21 Lower Camden Street and 97 Upper Leeson Street. The 1916 Proclamation of the Irish Republic was written in her home and during the Rising she supplied food to the Volunteers. She and her daughter Nancy were involved in the Irish National Aid and Volunteer Dependants' Fund (INAAVDF), which helped support the families of incarcerated Republicans after the Rising and during the War of Independence. In 1920 she was elected to Dublin Corporation. She supported the Treaty and helped set up Cumann na Saoirse, the pro-Treaty women's organisation, becoming its vice-president. From 1922 until 1936 she was a Free State senator and also a member of Cumann na nGaedheal. She died in 1941. (*Courtesy of Kilmainham Gaol Archives, 08PC-1B52-16*)

Maud Gonne was born in Aldershot, England in 1865. Her mother died when she was young and she was raised by a governess, spending some time in France. Her father, Thomas, was an officer in the British Army and when he was posted to the Curragh Camp in the early 1880s Maud accompanied him to Ireland.

Although she came from a privileged background, Maud dedicated her life to Ireland. She did things on her own terms and this can be seen in both her public and personal life – wherever she saw injustice she tried to change things. She joined the Land League and campaigned for tenant farmers being evicted from their homes, as well as highlighting the terrible conditions the 'Fenian Dynamitards' were enduring in prison for their part in the Fenian dynamite campaign in which a number of high profile buildings were targeted in a bombing campaign in England in the 1880s. Her efforts on their behalf helped secure their early release from prison. She was also involved in the Gaelic literary revival.

Maud divided her time between Ireland and France. She had two children with French journalist Lucien Millevoye: George in 1891, who died in infancy, and Iseult in 1895. The fact that she was not married did not prevent her from continuing her public work, going on lecture tours and also editing the Parisian newspaper *L'Irlande Libre*, a radical separatist paper which included Irish affairs.

In 1903 Maud married Major John MacBride, who fought with the Boers in the Irish Brigade against the British. They shared the same political views but the marriage did not last. They had one son, Seán, who, like his parents, devoted his life to the cause of Irish independence and also to those suffering human rights abuses, helping to set up Amnesty International. (*Courtesy of Mercier Archive*)

Realising that there was no outlet for Irish women to be politically active, Maud Gonne formed Inghinidhe na hÉireann (Daughters of Ireland) in 1900. This photograph shows her (*centre holding the banner*) with members of Inghinidhe *c.* 1905–6. The organisation's objective was to promote all things Irish and the members were

not afraid to put themselves in harm's way to prove their point. In 1903 they were successful in canvassing the councillors of Dublin not to provide a loyal address when King Edward VII came to visit Ireland. (*Courtesy of Kilmainham Gaol Archives, 13PO-1B54-14*)

One of Inghinidhe na hÉireann's most pro-active and forward-thinking achievements was the promotion of education amongst the poorer classes of Dublin city. They wanted to show those children that other choices were available when they were older. In the case of young boys they were particularly keen to show them that options existed besides joining the British Army. The members provided free classes to children over nine and promoted the Irish language and history, subjects that were not deemed to be relevant by the authorities. One of these classes is shown above, with a group of teachers from Inghinidhe na hÉireann opposite. They gave these children a sense of pride and place, and many of them went on to fight in the Irish revolution. The classes were held at Inghinidhe headquarters, initially at 196 Great Brunswick Street and later at North Great Georges Street. (*Courtesy of the National Library of Ireland*)

Realising that the organisation was not only socially aware, but had a penchant for taking on difficult tasks, Inghinidhe was approached by the Augustinian Order based in John's Lane off Thomas Street to help provide meals to the children of the area, which was at that time one of the poorest areas in Dublin. With the help of the Little Flower Penny Dinners in Meath Street, Inghinidhe distributed proper meals to the children. The Little Flower Penny Dinners was a charitable organisation set up in 1912 on the instigation of the parish priest in Meath Street, which sought to feed the poorer people in the Liberties. For many this would be the only meal they would receive in a day. The children paid a penny or halfpenny if they could, but no child went unfed. Later the payment came from local rates. (*Courtesy of the National Library of Ireland*)

Born in 1884, Helena Molony joined Inghinidhe na hÉireann in 1903 and in that same year canvassed against King Edward VII's visit to Ireland. A close associate of Maud Gonne, she effectively took over the running of Inghinidhe when Gonne was in France. She was a teacher for Inghinidhe and was elected honorary secretary, holding that position until 1910. In 1907 she helped set up Inghinidhe's newspaper *Bean na hÉireann* and became its editor. In 1911 she was arrested for protesting against King George V's visit to Ireland and was sentenced to one month in prison for throwing stones at a sign depicting the King's image. After spending some time in France, on her return to Ireland in December 1914 she joined the Abbey Theatre, having been a member and taking part in many of the theatrical productions of its forerunner, the National Players Society.

A friend of James Connolly, she became involved with the Labour movement in 1913. She assisted Delia Larkin, who had set up a co-op and shirt-making factory on Eden Quay employing girls who had been unable to get work because of their involvement in the Lockout. She was asked by Connolly to organise these girls into a female subsidiary of the ICA. She was a member of the City Hall garrison during the Rising and after her arrest she was held in Kilmainham Gaol and Mountjoy Prison before being sent to Lewes and Aylesbury prisons in England. She was released in December 1916. (*Courtesy of James Langton*)

Sinéad de Valera was born Jane Flanagan in Balbriggan on 1 June 1878. One of eleven children born to Laurence and Margaret Flanagan, she moved with the family to Dublin at the age of seven. Her interest in Irish affairs began during the centenary celebrations of the 1798 Rebellion after which she joined the Gaelic League. She changed her name to Sinéad Ní Fhlannagáin and began teaching in Francis Xavier's school in Dublin. She was also a member of Inghinidhe na hÉireann and helped found the Abbey Theatre. It was as a teacher for the Gaelic League in Parnell Square that she met Éamon de Valera. Although he was her pupil, they married in January 1910 at St Paul's Church, Arran Quay. Sinéad was very supportive of her husband's Republican activities in 1916, despite the fact that they had a young family and she was pregnant again. Éamon was sentenced to death after the Rising but this sentence was later commuted to penal servitude for life and he was sent to prison in England. The couple's fifth child, Ruairi, was born in November 1916 and it would be almost seven months before Éamon saw his newborn son, having been released in the general amnesty in June 1917. (*Courtesy of Kilmainham Gaol Archives, 13PC-1B14-12*)

Constance Gore-Booth was born in Sligo in 1868 into a wealthy Anglo-Irish family and was presented to the court of Queen Victoria in 1887. In 1900 she married Count Casimir Markievicz, with whom she had a daughter, Maeve, in 1901. The couple influenced each other in their political outlook and although the marriage was not to last they remained close. She joined Inghinidhe na hÉireann in 1907 arriving at her first meeting wearing an evening gown. She also wrote for their newspaper *Bean na hÉireann*. In 1909 she helped set up Na Fianna Éireann with Bulmer Hobson. Their aim was to establish an Irish equivalent to Baden Powell's Boy Scouts, to promote the Irish language, and to train its members in the use of signalling and drill. Many, if not all, went on to participate in the Irish revolution in the coming years. Initially Na Fianna did not have a premises where they could train and practise, but Markievicz lived in Surrey House in Rathmines, a property with a miniature rifle range, which she made available to them as their unofficial headquarters. They used Surrey House until they moved to permanent headquarters in D'Olier Street. (*Courtesy of Mercier Archive*)

Nellie Gifford, born in 1880, was a member of the Women's Section of the ICA and was involved in the 1913 Lockout. As she was a domestic economy instructor, her skills were put to good use in the soup kitchens and also training the ICA in how to cook in the field. Posing as Jim Larkin's niece she helped get him into the Imperial Hotel from where he was able to give his famous speech on 31 August 1913, which led to the baton charge by the police on the crowds outside. She was wounded by the police when they entered the room to arrest Larkin. (*Courtesy of James Langton*)

OVERLEAF

Delia Larkin (*front row, fourth from left*) was born in Toxteth, Liverpool, in 1878 and was the younger sister of James Larkin, founder of the Irish Transport and General Workers' Union (ITGWU). She was heavily influenced by her older brother and came to live with him and his family in Dublin. She was trained as a teacher but also ran a hotel for a short time in Co. Down. She became involved in the trade union movement in 1911 and helped set up the Irish Women Workers' Union (IWWU) in September 1911. Its aim was to improve women's rights in the workplace. Its members also wanted suffrage for women and highlighted other social issues affecting them. The women in the photograph were just some of its members who suffered terms of imprisonment for the cause. They are seated on the steps of Liberty Hall holding a board proclaiming them 'Freedom's Martyrs'.

In November 1913, during the Lockout, James Larkin went to England, leaving Delia to run Liberty Hall, the headquarters of the ITGWU. She organised soup kitchens there for starving workers and their families. After the Lockout ended she discovered that many of the women who had been out on strike were unable to find work. To combat this she set up a shirt-making factory close to Liberty Hall on Eden Quay and gave the girls work.

In 1921 she married Patrick Colgan, a member of the ICA, and they lived in Gardiner Street and later Ballsbridge. She died in 1949, aged seventy-one, and is buried in Glasnevin Cemetery. (*Courtesy of the National Library of Ireland*)

IRISH
WOMEN
I W
W U
WORKERS
UNION

"Freedom's Mar[...]
Members of the [...]
Women Workers
who suffered
terms of imprison[...]
in the cause [...]
Labour"

Rosie Hackett was born in Dublin in 1893. An ardent trade unionist, in 1911 she co-founded the IWWU with Delia Larkin. She worked in Jacob's Biscuit Factory and on 1 September 1913, when two of the female workers in Jacob's were dismissed from their jobs for refusing to remove their union badges, Rosie, along with over 300 female workers in Jacob's, refused to remove their badges in sympathy with their colleagues. They were also fired. In all 310 women were 'Locked Out' of Jacob's. During the Lockout Rosie helped run the soup kitchen in Liberty Hall. Failing to get her job back after the Lockout ended, she found work as a clerk in the IWWU shop set up by Delia Larkin to help those women who could not regain employment. Rosie also sold items in the shop and trained as a printer on the printing press used by Liberty Hall. This work brought her into close contact with James Connolly and as a result she became involved with the ICA, taking part in route marches with the other women at night and helping to make first aid kits and knapsacks for the men. She also assisted Dr Kathleen Lynn in her surgery in Liberty Hall. During the Rising she fought in St Stephen's Green and the College of Surgeons. After the surrender she was arrested and taken to Kilmainham Gaol and when she was released she returned to the ruined Liberty Hall and helped reorganise the ICA. She joined the Fairview Branch of Cumann na mBan in 1919, helping to train the women in first aid, but left the organisation in 1920. Committed to the rights of the working classes, she helped to re-organise the IWWU. She died in 1976, aged eighty-four and is buried in Glasnevin Cemetery. (*Courtesy of Eamon Murphy*)

Lizzie Merrigan (*right*) and an unidentified girl, *c.* 1915–16, in Clan na nGaedheal uniforms. The Clan na nGaedheal Girl Scouts were set up by Countess Markievicz and May and Liz Kelly in 1910. It was to be an independent organisation solely for girls, focusing on preparing the young women of Ireland to help the nationalist cause. Its members were not allowed to be members of any other political organisation. Many of the girls who had joined Clan na nGaedheal went on to work for the Republican cause in the coming years. Like her older sister, Nellie, Lizzie became a member of Cumann na mBan and took the anti-Treaty side during the Civil War. She was arrested with her sister in March 1923, during a Free State crackdown on the anti-Treaty movement, and imprisoned in Kilmainham Gaol. She died in 1926; she was only twenty-four years old. (*Courtesy of Kilmainham Gaol Archives, 18PO-1B53-17*)

Dr Kathleen Lynn, shown here holding Barbara MacDonagh (with Thomas and Donagh MacDonagh behind her and an unidentified woman to the right), was born in 1874 in Mallaghfarry, Co. Mayo, and moved to Longford when she was nine. In 1899 she received her medical degree from the Royal University and undertook a fellowship at the College of Surgeons. She worked in private practice at her home in Belgrave Road and through her distant cousin Countess Markievicz she met Helena Molony, whom she treated for illness. As a result of their meeting Lynn became involved in the nationalist movement, joining the Women's Section of the ICA. She gave lectures in first aid to them, and later to Cumann na mBan, as well as running a surgery from Liberty Hall. It was in these early days of the ICA that she met Madeleine Ffrench-Mullen, who not only became her lifelong friend but also shared her vision of trying to make life better for the ordinary working classes and their families. (*Courtesy of Martin O'Dwyer*)

Áine Ceannt was born Frances O'Brennan in Dublin in September 1880 and was the youngest of four girls. She joined the Central Branch of the Gaelic League, after which she changed her name to Áine, and it was through the League that she met Éamonn Ceannt. They married in James' Street church in 1905 and their son Rónán was born in June 1906. She and Éamonn shared the same political views – he joined the Irish Volunteers upon its inception in 1913, and she and her sister Lily joined the Central Branch of Cumann na mBan when it was founded in 1914. After the Easter Rising she was elected both honorary treasurer and vice-president of the organisation. Éamonn, as commandant of the 4th Battalion, Dublin Brigade, Irish Volunteers, was executed for his part in the Easter Rising. (*Courtesy of Kilmainham Gaol Archives, 17PC-1B52-04*)

The eldest of the MacSwiney children, Mary was born in Surrey, England, in 1872, before the family moved to Cork in 1878. Mary went to university in Cambridge, qualifying as a teacher. When her mother died in 1904 she returned to Cork. Through her brother Terence she became involved in the nationalist movement and was a founder member of the Gaelic League and Cumann na mBan in Cork, of which she was elected president. She was a teacher in St Angela's High School in Cork but lost her job there as a result of her arrest after the Easter Rising. Together with her younger sister Annie, she set up St Ita's school for girls in Cork city. (*Courtesy of the National Library of Ireland*)

May Conlon came from Shandon in Cork city and, with her sister Lil, was among the founding members of the Cork Branch of Cumann na mBan. Like all members of Cumann na mBan, their work included drill practice, first aid and collecting funds for the Volunteers. She founded the Shandon Branch of Cumann na mBan in January 1918 and was elected honorary secretary. In 1919 she was also elected as honorary secretary to Cork District Council, Cumann na mBan, and the executive of Cumann na mBan, Cork as well as being a member of the headquarters staff. (*Courtesy of Cork County Museum*)

Molly Childers (*left*), née Osgood, was born in Boston in 1877. She was involved in a skating accident when she was a child which left her a cripple. She met her future husband, Erskine Childers, in 1903 while he was visiting Boston. They fell in love and a year later they were married, after which they moved to London and had three sons. Molly was a nationalist and when Mary Spring Rice approached Erskine with plans to smuggle weapons into Ireland, Molly was fully supportive and was a secretary of the committee that planned the operation. She and Mary Spring Rice took part in the Howth gun-running in July 1914 as can be seen in this picture taken at the time on board the *Asgard*, the yacht belonging to the Childers that was used to smuggle the weapons to Howth.

In 1919 the Childers family settled in Ireland where Molly helped her husband in his work as director of propaganda for the Republican movement during the later stages of the War of Independence. She sheltered IRA men on the run and was a trustee of the White Cross while also helping distribute funds from the Dáil Loan, set up in 1919 in order to finance Dáil Éireann. She and her husband opposed the Treaty. Erskine Childers continued to work as a propagandist for the anti-Treaty side and was captured in November 1922. He was executed in Beggars Bush Barracks under the Special Powers Act introduced by the Provisional Government during the Civil War. Following her husband's death, Molly carried on his work as a propagandist for the anti-Treaty forces. She died in 1964, aged eighty-seven.

Mary Spring Rice (*right*) was born in 1880 to Lord Mounteagle and his wife Elizabeth at Mount Trenchard, Foynes, Co. Limerick. She joined the Gaelic League and was a member of branches in Limerick, Dublin and London. She was interested in politics from an early age and was active in promoting the co-op movement. She joined Sinn Féin and was later a member of the Glin Branch of Cumann na mBan. It was because of her suggestion that the Howth gun-running took place and she was a member of the committee that raised funds for the expedition, raising £2,000 herself.

While in Cumann na mBan Mary lectured in first aid and other essential duties that the women would have to undertake. During the War of Independence her home was always open to the Volunteers of the West Limerick Brigade who were on the run. She died in 1924 in Wales after a long illness, aged forty-four, and is buried near her home in Loughill, Mount Trenchard, Co. Limerick. (*Courtesy of Mercier Archive*)

In this photograph Mrs Teresa Reddin, Central Branch, Cumann na mBan, leads the funeral procession for the victims of the Bachelor's Walk shootings in her pony and trap in July 1914. In a mark of open defiance, the women in the procession, mainly members of Cumann na mBan, wear large white ostrich feathers in their hats. The feather was a symbol of cowardice and the women proudly wore them in protest, highlighting the fact that the people the army had killed and wounded on 26 July were not soldiers, but unarmed civilians.

Teresa Reddin (née Shiels) was born in Dungooley, Forkhill, Co. Louth, in 1869. In 1890 she married John J. Reddin and the couple moved to Artane, Co. Dublin. Teresa was very interested in Irish culture, heritage and politics, and she was determined to contribute to the Irish nationalist movement. When Cumann na mBan was founded in April 1914, she immediately joined the Central Branch, of which she was elected treasurer. She was later appointed to the executive. She was close friends with Mrs Pearse, and her twin boys Kenneth and Norman were educated in St Enda's school, Rathfarnham.

Her home in Artane was put at the disposal of Na Fianna, who would regularly use the grounds for their training camps. One of Teresa's duties as a member of Cumann na mBan was to teach first aid to the women. She did not take part in the Easter Rising but three of her sons who were in the Volunteers did fight and after the surrender they were arrested and deported to Stafford Gaol in England and later to Frongoch internment camp in Wales. Teresa's politics were well known to the authorities and in the aftermath of the Rising she was placed under house arrest. She remained a member of the executive of Cumann na mBan and continued with her involvement in the organisation right through the War of Independence. (*Courtesy of Kilmainham Gaol Archives, 16PO-1A23-09*)

Mary Lawlor (née O'Carroll), was born in Dolphin's Barn Lane, Dublin, in 1899. Dolly, as she was more commonly known, came from a Republican family and her father, Peter, was a Fenian. When Dolly was young the family moved to Manor Street, where her father and mother, Annie, ran a general store. Her brothers Liam, Jim and Peter were all members of Na Fianna Éireann and joined the Irish Volunteers upon its inception, becoming members of 'A' Company, 1st Battalion, Dublin Brigade, Irish Volunteers.

Dolly joined the Gaelic League when she was thirteen years old and also joined Cumann na mBan in 1915. She asked Sally Neary of the Central Branch of Cumann na mBan, based in Parnell Square, if another branch could be established, and as a result the Colmcille Branch of Cumann na mBan was set up in Blackhall Street. She was only sixteen years old. (*Courtesy of Bernadine and Audrey Flanagan*)

Annie Derham in her Cumann na mBan uniform. She joined the Central Branch of Cumann na mBan upon its inception in 1914 and was active during the Rising. She died in January 1918 in her home in Connaught Street, Dublin. (*Courtesy of Kilmainham Gaol Archives, 17PC-1A41-30a*)

Members of Cumann na mBan at Fairview in 1914. Standing (*left to right*): Gertie Colley, Esther Wisely, Statia Twomey, unidentified, Amee MacDonald. Seated, second from right, is Annie White. Unfortunately it has not been possible to identify the other women. (*Courtesy of Kilmainham Gaol Archives, 13PC-1B52-25*)

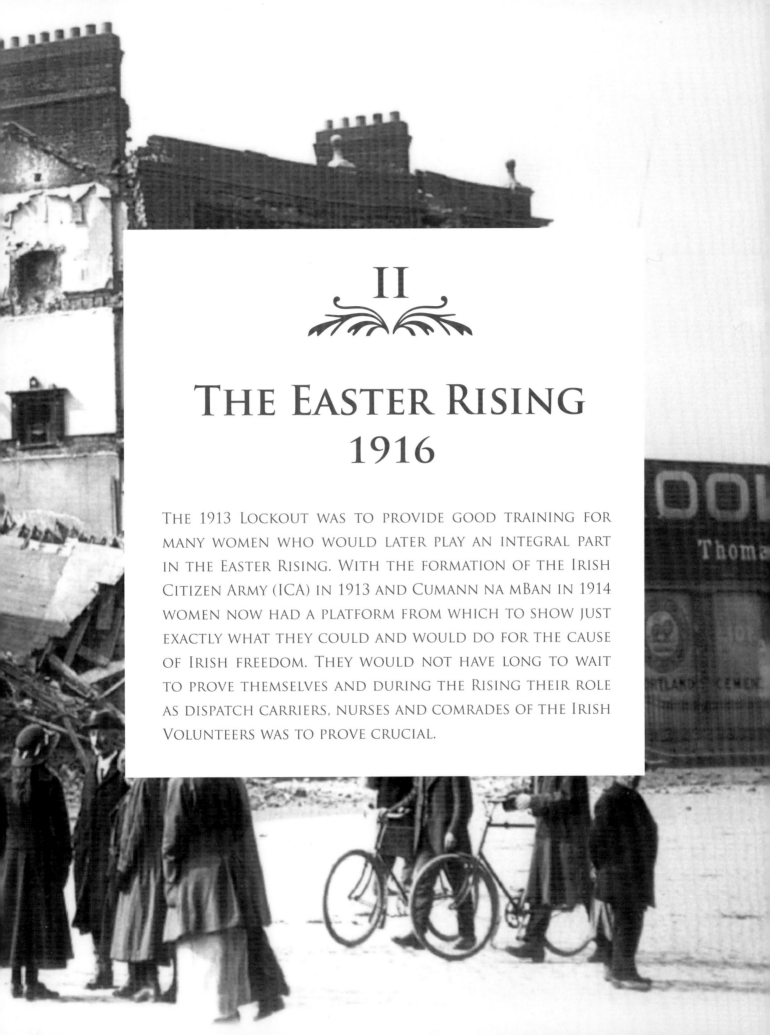

II

THE EASTER RISING 1916

THE 1913 LOCKOUT WAS TO PROVIDE GOOD TRAINING FOR MANY WOMEN WHO WOULD LATER PLAY AN INTEGRAL PART IN THE EASTER RISING. WITH THE FORMATION OF THE IRISH CITIZEN ARMY (ICA) IN 1913 AND CUMANN NA MBAN IN 1914 WOMEN NOW HAD A PLATFORM FROM WHICH TO SHOW JUST EXACTLY WHAT THEY COULD AND WOULD DO FOR THE CAUSE OF IRISH FREEDOM. THEY WOULD NOT HAVE LONG TO WAIT TO PROVE THEMSELVES AND DURING THE RISING THEIR ROLE AS DISPATCH CARRIERS, NURSES AND COMRADES OF THE IRISH VOLUNTEERS WAS TO PROVE CRUCIAL.

Molly O'Reilly was from Gardiner Street, Dublin and at the age of nine she went to Liberty Hall to learn Irish dancing. There she first heard James Connolly speak and was enthralled. During the Lockout, aged only eleven, with Connolly's children Roddy and Aideen, she ran messages from Connolly in Liberty Hall to the strikers and also helped in the soup kitchens and collected money. After the Howth gun-running she hid some of the weapons in her house in Gardiner Street. All of this activity was unknown to her father, who was a staunch supporter of the crown.

The week before the Easter Rising James Connolly sent for her to carry out the special assignment of hoisting the ICA flag of green with a gold harp over Liberty Hall, an honour she proudly accepted. She was only fourteen years old. When the Rising began she marched to City Hall with Seán Connolly's garrison and carried messages to and from the GPO until City Hall was taken by British forces on Tuesday. She evaded arrest and after the Rising went to England as a student nurse, but returned home in 1917 and joined Cumann na mBan.

During the War of Independence she was responsible for arranging safe houses for Volunteers on the run. She worked in Bon Bouche in Dawson Street, a coffee shop owned by Countess Markievicz and Charlotte Despard. This employment enabled her to carry on her Republican work unhindered, including delivering dispatches to IRA units around the country as well as transporting arms and gelignite to the IRA in Dalkey, the unit she was assigned to. Often this work was carried out late at night and she had more than one close encounter with the Black and Tans.

In the course of the Irish Civil War she took the anti-Treaty side and was arrested in 1923. During her imprisonment she went on hunger strike and after sixteen days on the strike she was released. She later married Ned Corcoran who was a member of the 5th Battalion (Engineers), Dublin Brigade, IRA. They had five children, four boys and one girl, whom she named Constance after her good friend Countess Markievicz. (*Courtesy of Constance Corcoran*)

Madeleine Ffrench-Mullen was born in Malta in 1880, where her father was a member of the Royal Navy. On his retirement the family moved to Ireland. Socially and politically aware at a young age, Madeleine devoted her life to helping those in need. She was a member of Inghinidhe na hÉireann, writing a children's column for their paper *Bean na hÉireann* and helping with their school dinners initiative. She became involved in the labour movement and helped in the soup kitchens during the Lockout after which she joined the ICA where she met Dr Kathleen Lynn. When Cumann na mBan was established Madeleine joined the organisation and was a member of the Central Branch. During the Rising she served with the St Stephen's Green/College of Surgeons garrison and was in command of fifteen women whose duties included commandeering vehicles, guarding the entrances to the park, tending to the wounded and also feeding the garrison. After the surrender she was taken to Kilmainham Gaol and later to Mountjoy Prison. She was released on 4 June.

After the Easter Rising Madeleine found work with the Connolly Co-operative Society, which was established to help find work for those who had lost their jobs because they fought in the Rising. Aware of the terrible social conditions that prevailed in Dublin, Madeleine was determined to improve the living conditions of the poor, particularly the children. Madeleine and Kathleen Lynn believed that in order to improve the life expectancy of the poor children of Dublin, the city needed a hospital dedicated to the treatment of childhood illnesses. A committee was set up and St Ultan's Infant Hospital in Charlemont Street opened its doors in 1919, the first hospital of its kind in the country. During the War of Independence it would seem she was also involved in gathering intelligence, as she was arrested for keeping a military patrol under surveillance.

Madeleine opposed the Anglo-Irish Treaty and during the Civil War assisted anti-Treaty forces any way she could, gathering intelligence and tending to wounded men. In 1935 she was a founding member of the Joint Committee of Women's Societies and Social Workers and was also at that time a member of the Rathmines Urban District Council. Through her membership of the Ultan's Utility Society and the Charlemont Utility Society, Madeleine helped to house people who had lived in the tenements in new homes. Madeleine Ffrench-Mullen died in 1944. She was sixty-four. (*Reproduced by kind permission of the College of Physicians*)

Leslie Price was born in Dublin in 1893, the third of six children. She came from a nationalist family and her brothers Éamon and Seán were members of the Irish Volunteers. She and Éamon were members of the Gaelic League and in August 1915 she joined the Central Branch of Cumann na mBan having been inspired by the funeral of O'Donovan Rossa. She began teaching in the Sisters of Charity National School on Gardiner Street.

On Easter Monday 1916 Leslie turned out for mobilisation and, despite receiving orders from Commandant Ned Daly to return home, she and some other girls decided to go to the GPO where she found her older brother, Éamon. Seán also fought in the Rising. Leslie was sent to the Hibernian Bank on O'Connell Street, which was under the command of Captain Thomas Weafer, whom she tried to save after he was fatally wounded. She returned to the GPO and carried dispatches from the GPO to the Fr Mathew Hall in Church Street. She was ordered by Tom Clarke to fetch a priest from the pro-cathedral to bring to the GPO, which she did successfully although under constant fire. She was in the evacuation party that brought the wounded from the GPO to Jervis Street Hospital and was arrested and taken to Broadstone Station, but was released soon after. (*Courtesy of Meda Ryan*)

Mary Coakley, née Matthews. Known as 'Red Mary', she was from Waterford Street in Dublin. Although not a member of Cumann na mBan, she was active during the Rising, acting as a dispatch carrier between the GPO and the College of Surgeons. She was married to Thomas Coakley and they had seven children, two girls and five boys. (*Courtesy of Molly Cunningham*)

Margaret Skinnider was born outside Glasgow in 1893 to Irish parents. She trained to be a teacher and joined the Glasgow Branch of Cumann na mBan, becoming adept in the use of weapons. In 1915 she came to Ireland and managed to smuggle in detonators for bombs which she kept in her hat. She returned to Glasgow but on Holy Thursday 1916 she came back to Ireland after she had been informed of the plans for the Rising. She joined the ICA as a dispatch carrier between the College of Surgeons and the GPO. During the fighting she was seriously wounded while involved in an attempt to try and set fire to buildings on Harcourt Street where British soldiers were stationed. She states in her pension application that a 'gunshot wound ¼ inch from spine [was] received in action about 2 am. Thursday, April 27th 1916 in Harcourt St while in charge of five men sent to take house on Harcourt St.' She was in hospital for seven weeks and was not arrested after her discharge so she returned to Glasgow and from there went on a lecture tour of America in 1917. Returning to Ireland she joined the Central Branch of Cumann na mBan. She took the anti-Treaty side during the Civil War and was a member of the executive of Cumann na mBan. She was arrested in November 1922 when found in possession of a revolver and was held in the North Dublin Union (NDU). Upon her release she resumed her work as a teacher and retired in 1961. She was a member of the Irish National Teachers' Organisation (INTO) and became its president in 1956. An advocate of women's rights, she was instrumental in helping get incremental salary scales for women and single men introduced. Margaret Skinnider died in October 1971 at the age of seventy-eight and is buried in Glasnevin Cemetery. (*Courtesy of James Langton*)

A member of the ICA, Constance Markievicz was Michael Mallin's second in command in St Stephen's Green and the College of Surgeons garrison during the 1916 Rising. When the surrender order came through from Patrick Pearse, she was arrested along with the rest of the garrison. This photograph shows her just after her court martial in Richmond Barracks. Sentenced to death for her part in the Rising, the government quickly realised that the execution of a woman would sway public opinion in favour of the rebels and so her sentence was commuted to life imprisonment. She was incarcerated in Kilmainham Gaol, Mountjoy Prison and later Aylesbury Prison in England, during which time she was re-elected as president of Cumann na mBan. (*Courtesy of the Michael Curran Collection*)

Before the Easter Rising Nellie Gifford set up a Public Employment Bureau with Marie Perolz in 6 Harcourt Street to find jobs for those Volunteers who came over from England to avoid conscription. Joseph Plunkett, her future brother-in-law, was looking for a secretary and she suggested Michael Collins for the job. During the Rising she was a member of the St Stephen's Green/College of Surgeons garrison. Arrested after the surrender, she was held in Richmond Barracks, Kilmainham Gaol and Mountjoy Prison, and was actually in Kilmainham at the time of her sister Grace's wedding to Plunkett, but was not allowed to attend the ceremony. After her release she went to America on a lecture tour to raise awareness about the Rising. She married Joseph Donnelly in 1918 and they had one daughter, Maeve. She and her daughter returned to Ireland in 1921. In later life she was a founding member of the Kilmainham Gaol Restoration Society. She died in 1971, aged ninety-one. (*Courtesy of Kilmainham Gaol Archives, 2012.0143*)

Elizabeth O'Farrell (*standing first on right*) was born in Dublin in 1883. She was educated at the Convent of the Sisters of Mercy, Townsend Street. She joined Inghinidhe na hÉireann in 1906 and became a member of the Inghinidhe Branch of Cumann na mBan upon its inception in 1914. Before the Rising she was one of the many women couriers who travelled around the country giving details of the plans for the mobilisation. She was herself sent to Galway. She was attached to the ICA during the Rising and served in the GPO carrying dispatches between the various outposts. She was chosen by Patrick Pearse not only to deliver the message to Brigadier General Lowe of the British forces regarding the surrender, but also to bring the surrender order to the Volunteer garrisons around the city. When she had completed this assignment she was arrested. She was taken to Ship Street Barracks and then to Kilmainham Gaol, where she was held for a short time.

Elizabeth was engaged to be married, but her fiancé lived abroad and she would not leave Ireland. She did, however, fulfil her lifelong dream to become a nurse and trained as a midwife in Holles Street Hospital. There is a plaque to her memory there and a medal known as the Elizabeth O'Farrell medal is presented each year to the student who achieves the second highest marks in midwifery. Elizabeth O'Farrell died in 1957 at the age of seventy-four and is buried in Glasnevin Cemetery. (*Courtesy of James Langton*)

Matilda or Tilly Simpson (*front row, second from right*) was from Goosegreen in Drumcondra, Dublin. She was a member of the Fairview Branch of Cumann na mBan and, with her sister Mollie and her brother Terence, participated in the Easter Rising. Tilly served in the GPO during Easter Week and helped take those wounded in the fighting to nearby Jervis Street Hospital.

During the War of Independence she helped collect money for the INAAVDF while also transporting ammunition for the 2nd Battalion, Dublin Brigade IRA. Tilly opposed the Treaty and during the Civil War she served in the anti-Treaty outposts in Moran's Hotel and the Gresham Hotel, treating those who were wounded. She was arrested and imprisoned in Kilmainham Gaol and the NDU. (*Courtesy of James Langton*)

Alice Cashel was born in Meath in 1878. She joined the Gaelic League in 1893 and went to live with her father in Cork when she was training to become a teacher. She was a member of Sinn Féin and helped set up the Cork Branch of Cumann na mBan with Mary and Annie MacSwiney – she was appointed secretary of the branch. In 1916 she was living in Limerick but was ordered by Tomás MacCurtain to return to Cork on Holy Thursday. It was Alice's job to obtain cars that were to be driven to Kerry so that the Volunteers could collect the arms that were due to be landed there. The day after she arrived in Cork she heard of the arrest of Roger Casement, who had come from Germany with the much-needed arms. With no weapons to collect and no orders forthcoming, Alice remained in Cork for the rest of Easter Week and returned to Limerick when the fighting in Dublin ended. (*Courtesy of Mark Humphrys*)

Brigid Mahon, Dublin, wearing her Cumann na mBan uniform. Brigid was a member of the Inghinidhe Branch of Cumann na mBan and took part in the Easter Rising carrying dispatches between the GPO, Boland's Mills and the College of Surgeons. She opposed the Treaty and during the Civil War she was active in the anti-Treaty IRA garrison in the Gresham Hotel and later St Stephen's Green, where she carried out first-aid duties. (*Courtesy of Stephen Byrne*)

Marcella Cosgrave was born in Dublin in 1875. From an early age she was an advocate of both women's rights and Ireland's rights as a nation. She was a member of the Ladies' Land League, joined Inghinidhe na hÉireann upon its inception and was later a founding member of Cumann na mBan. In the 1911 census she made a stand by signing her name in Irish as Marsála Ní Coisghraighe. She was a member of the Marrowbone Lane Distillery garrison during the Easter Rising, and served as quartermaster of Cumann na mBan in the garrison. Following the surrender she and her comrades were taken to Richmond Barracks and then Kilmainham Gaol, but were released after ten days. She lived on George's Quay beside Julia Maher, a fellow member of Cumann na mBan. She died in 1938, aged sixty-three. (*Courtesy of Kilmainham Gaol Archives, 2012.0131*)

Emily (*standing*) and Essie Elliot. The sisters were from Gardiner's Place, Dublin and were both members of the Central Branch of Cumann na mBan. When the Rising began, Emily was initially stationed in Reis's Chambers, O'Connell Street. This building was a key position for the Volunteers as it held the Wireless School and the plan was to establish communications abroad and report what was happening. She and the other women stationed there had to run the gauntlet between Reis's and Volunteer headquarters in the GPO in order to get food for the garrison in Reis's.

While delivering dispatches with Eilís Ní Riain, Emily decided to collect her sister from home and the three women returned to Reis's after which they were sent to reinforce the garrison in the Four Courts/Church Street area. They reported to the Fr Mathew Hall, which was a first aid station, and were given white armlets and helped carry out first aid on the wounded. Emily and Eilís managed to escape from the hall on the morning of the surrender, 30 April 1916. They were not arrested and returned home. (*Courtesy of James Langton*)

Mary 'Mamie' Kilmartin was born in Stoneybatter, Dublin, in 1895 and came from a Republican family. Both she and her brother Paddy were involved in the Republican movement. She joined the Colmcille Branch of Cumann na mBan, while Paddy joined the Irish Volunteers. Before the Rising she helped prepare first-aid kits and food rations for the Volunteers and during the Rising she was attached to the Four Courts garrison where she carried out first-aid duties, both at the Courts and at Skipper's Alley nearby. Paddy fought in the GPO and Phibsboro.

After the surrender Mamie evaded arrest. In 1917 she married Patrick Joseph Stephenson, who was a member of the Volunteers and had fought in the Mendicity Institution under Seán Heuston, as well as in the GPO, in 1916. The best man at their wedding was fellow Volunteer Seán McLoughlin, who had fought beside Stephenson during the Rising. Due to her new status as a newly-wed, Mamie did not actively participate in the events of the coming years. She was now a wife and soon became a mother, a responsibility she put above everything else. Although she wasn't active she did support her husband, who continued his involvement with the Volunteers during the War of Independence. Mamie and Patrick would eventually have five sons. (*Courtesy of Pat and Jim Stephenson and Dave Kilmartin*)

Mary Cullen was born in Reginald Street, the Liberties, Dublin, in 1896. During the Easter Rising she was sent with Bridget Grace, on the orders of James Connolly, with dispatches and food to the Volunteer garrison in No. 25 Northumberland Road. They could not enter the premises as the house was barricaded, but they did manage to inform Lieutenant Michael Malone and Seamus Grace, Bridget's brother, that the expected British reinforcements had landed in Dun Laoghaire and were going to be entering the city right through their positions. Mary's sisters, Julia and Nan, both joined the Éamonn Ceannt Branch of Cumann na mBan upon its formation after the Easter Rising. (*Courtesy of Stephen Carey*)

Rose McGuinness was a member of the Central Branch of Cumann na mBan and took part in the Easter Rising. She served with the Four Courts garrison carrying dispatches between the Courts and the surrounding outposts. She was wounded during the fighting in the Four Courts by some falling glass. She evaded capture after the garrison surrendered, but her health never fully recovered and in January 1919 she died. (*Courtesy of the McGuinness Collection*)

Mary Josephine (Min) Ryan was born in Wexford in 1884 and was the sixth of the twelve children of John and Eliza Ryan (eight girls and four boys). Education was of utmost importance to their parents and all the girls were educated in Loreto College, Gorey, after which they all went to university in Dublin. Min studied French, German and English at the Royal University in Dublin, spent time in Germany and France, and on graduating went to teach in London where she met many young Irish people with a similar political outlook to her own. She returned to Dublin in 1914 and got a job teaching in the Technical School in Rathmines. She lived with her sisters Phyllis (the youngest sister) and Mary Kate (Kit) in 19 Ranelagh Road. Min was a founding member of Cumann na mBan and later was appointed secretary of the organisation. Kit and another sister, Agnes, were also members, while their brother Jim, a medical student at the time, joined the Irish Volunteers. Min was extremely close to Seán MacDiarmada – he said himself that she was the one he would most likely have married, and before the Rising he sent her to Wexford with dispatches. She was then sent back to Wexford by Eoin MacNeill with the order countermanding the manoeuvres that would signal the start of the Rising.

Returning to Dublin in time for the Rising, Min, with Phyllis and Jim, went to the GPO on Easter Monday. She and Phyllis acted as messengers to and from the GPO. Neither was arrested but Kit and another sister, Ellen (Nell), who had not taken part, were arrested and held in Kilmainham Gaol before being transferred to England. Nell was not released from prison in England until October and upon her release returned to Wexford, joined Sinn Féin and was put in charge of Cumann na mBan in the county. Min was sent to America to report to John Devoy, leader of Clan na Gael about the Rising. Throughout this time and the War of Independence, Min was a member of the executive of Cumann na mBan. (*Courtesy of Elisabet Berney*)

Nora Connolly was born in Edinburgh in 1893 and was very close to her father James. When she was only eight years old he took her on a lecture tour of Scotland. The family moved to America in 1904 and she helped him with his paper *The Harp*. They returned to Ireland in 1910 and a year later they settled on the Falls Road in Belfast. She and her sister Ina joined the 'Betsy Gray Sluagh' of Na Fianna, the only girls' branch of the organisation, where she was chief officer. She and Ina took part in the Howth gun-running in 1914.

On Easter Saturday Nora and Ina went to Coalisland, Co. Tyrone, to meet with the Volunteers who were ordered to mobilise there. Whilst there they received word of MacNeill's countermanding order. The girls returned to Dublin where their father told them that the planned action would go ahead the next day. On Monday Nora and Ina were sent back to Tyrone by Patrick Pearse to inform the Volunteers that the Rising would go ahead. This they did, but only a small number of Volunteers turned out and no action took place. Nora and Ina tried to return to Dublin on Friday, but due to the fighting there they were unable to get back by train and had to walk from Dundalk. By the time they got back the Rising was over. Nora had this photo of herself in uniform taken as a joke for her father and signed it 'Your loving son'. He had a copy of it in his wallet at the time of the surrender and the British thought he had two sons as she looked so authentic.

After her father's execution it fell on Nora to provide for the family. She went to America and spoke about the situation in Ireland. There she met Seamus O'Brien, her future husband. She returned to Ireland in 1917 and helped with the general election in 1918. She was on the anti-Treaty side during the Civil War. She and Seamus were only newlyweds when they both fought in Dublin: she was stationed at Tara Hall and Seamus at the Gresham Hotel. They were arrested in late 1922. Nora was imprisoned in the NDU and Kilmainham Gaol, while Seamus was in Mountjoy Prison. Upon their release they ran a newsagency in Rialto, Dublin. They were both members of the Labour Party. They had no children and Seamus died in 1962. In 1966 Nora received an Honorary Doctorate of Law for her services to Ireland and became a senator. She was also a member of the Kilmainham Gaol Restoration Society. She wrote four books about her father and the Irish struggle. She died in 1981 at the age of eighty-eight. (*Courtesy of Kilmainham Gaol Archives, 17PC-1B52-06*)

Ina Connolly (*shown here with Archie Heron*) was born in 1896, the fourth child of James and Lily Connolly. When the family moved to Belfast in 1911 she and her older sister, Nora, joined the 'Betsy Gray Sluagh' of Na Fianna, of which Ina later became secretary. She was a member of the Gaelic League and regularly attended Irish classes at St Mary's Hall on the Fall's Road.

During the 1913 Lockout Ina helped collect money in Belfast for the strike fund in order to help the families of those on strike. She and Nora would regularly make trips from Belfast to Dublin and in April 1914 Ina attended the inaugural meeting of Cumann na mBan in Wynn's Hotel, Dublin. The sisters also took part in the Howth gun-running in July 1914 after which Ina had to transport some of the weapons to Belfast. She also took part in the funeral procession of O'Donovan Rossa in August 1915. While in Belfast she was a regular participant in the anti-recruiting campaign which had begun in opposition to the First World War. Her work entailed putting up posters around the city and selling nationalist newspapers. She was in Dublin with Nora when they were asked by Patrick Pearse to deliver a dispatch on Easter Monday to the Volunteers who would mobilise in Co. Tyrone, telling them that the Rising would go ahead. Ina was sent to Sixmilecross and Clogher, while Nora stayed in Coalisland. Ina completed her task successfully and until Friday of Easter Week, she was engaged with the Volunteers in Clogher moving ammunition and medical supplies, after which she returned to Dublin with Nora.

In 1918 Ina moved to London, where for two years she was actively engaged in helping the Republican cause by working with the London IRA. She was a member of the Irish Self-Determination League and regularly spoke at meetings highlighting Ireland's demand for independence. In the March 1920 by-election held in Stockport she actively campaigned for William O'Brien, a trade union organiser who was imprisoned in Wormwood Scrubs and was on hunger strike. She was also at this time working for Michael Collins, delivering messages from him to O'Brien.

Ina Connolly returned to Ireland in 1920. She opposed the Treaty and when the Civil War began in June 1922 she and Nora set up a first aid station in Tara Hall, Gloucester Street. They had little or no equipment and were forced to raid a chemist's for essential supplies. She also carried dispatches between the Republican outposts and their headquarters in the Hammam Hotel. She was not arrested in the Civil War. Ina later married Archie Heron, a veteran of the Volunteers and IRA. (*Courtesy of Kilmainham Gaol Archives, 17PC-1B52-06*)

This photograph shows sixty women from Cumann na mBan, the ICA and the Clan na nGaedheal Girl Scouts who took part in the Easter Rising. It was taken in the summer of 1916 in the garden of the house of Mrs Ely O'Carroll, Peter's Place, Dublin, where a meeting of the INAAVDF was held.

Front row (*left to right*): Madeleine Ffrench-Mullen, Brigid Foley, Dr Kathleen Lynn.

Second row: A. Tobin (*standing*), Rose MacNamara, Kathleen Kenny, Mary Joe Walsh, unidentified, Mrs Lawless, Jenny Milner, Eileen Walsh, K. Kennedy, May Byrne, Annie Cooney, Nora O'Daly (*standing*).

Third row: Aoife (Effie) Taafe (*standing*), May Moore, Kathleen Lane, Sarah Kealy, Gertie Colley, Mary O'Hanrahan, Amee (May) Wisely, Bridget Murtagh, Cilla S. Quigley, Julia Grenan, Statia Twomey, B. Walsh.

Fourth row: Marcella Cosgrave (*standing*), Mrs Kathleen Murphy (*standing*), Nora Thornton, Rose Mulally, Sheila O'Hanlon, Maria (Moira) Quigley, Margaret O'Flaherty, Josie McGowan, Eileen (Lily) Cooney, Josie O'Keeffe, Martha Kelly (*standing*), Máire Nic Shiúbhlaigh (*standing*), Elizabeth O'Farrell (*standing*), Lily O'Brennan (*standing*), Mary Murray (*standing*).

Fifth row: Bridget Foley, Lucy Agnes Smyth, Nora Foley, Pauline Morkan, Dolly O'Sullivan, Emily Elliot, Mary (Mollie) O'Sullivan, Matilda (Tilly) Simpson, Mrs Catherine Treston.

Sixth row: M. Kelly, Brigid Brady, Jane (Jinny) Shanahan, Mrs Katie Barrett, Rosie Hackett, Margaret (Máire) Ryan, Brigid Davis, Christina Keeley (née Caffrey), Patricia Hoey. (*Courtesy of Kilmainham Gaol Archives, 18PC-1B53-02*)

Christina Keeley (née Caffrey) was born in Dublin in 1898. She was a member of the ICA and during the Easter Rising she was attached to the St Stephen's Green/College of Surgeons garrison, where she carried dispatches, initially between the GPO and the College of Surgeons, and later to Jacob's Biscuit Factory. Christina evaded arrest after the surrender and three months after the Rising, on the orders of Madeleine Ffrench-Mullen and Helena Molony, she went to live in Glasgow, Scotland. Her task while there was to organise the collection and transportation of weapons from Glasgow to Ireland. She joined the Anne Devlin Branch of Cumann na mBan in Glasgow and worked as a dressmaker to support herself. In 1917 Christina began to transport not just revolvers, but also detonators and explosives, back to Ireland. She would undertake these journeys every two to three months. Throughout this time she also helped work for the INAAVDF, collecting and distributing money.

In 1918 Christina married James 'Jim' Keeley, who, like Christina, had fought in the Easter Rising. He worked as an iron-moulder and like Christina also transported weapons, concealing them in his melodeon. Their home in Woodside Avenue was used by the Glasgow IRA to store weapons and detonators. Christina and Jim returned to Dublin just after the Truce in July 1921 and settled in the East Wall/North Strand area. Christina did not take part in the Civil War. The couple had six children, three boys and three girls. Christina later worked as a wardrobe mistress for Mícheál MacLiammóir in the Abbey, Gate and the other big theatres in Dublin city. She died in 1976 at the age of seventy-eight. (*Courtesy of Gráinne Keeley*)

Many women suffered who were not actively involved in the Rising. Margaret Pearse's sons, Patrick and William, were both executed for their part in the Easter Rising. Patrick, as commander-in-chief of the Volunteers and signatory of the Proclamation was certain that he would be executed, but believed that William would at worst be put in prison. In his last letter to his mother on 3 May, Patrick wrote: 'I hope and believe that Willie and the St Enda's boys will be safe.' Mrs Pearse did not get to see Patrick before his execution on 3 May. She and her daughter Margaret were informed of his death later that morning by Fr Aloysius, who had visited Patrick before his execution. That night Mrs Pearse and Margaret were summoned to Kilmainham Gaol to see William, who had also been court-martialled. He was the only Volunteer to plead guilty and was sentenced to death, the execution to be carried out the next day. On 4 May 1916 William faced the firing squad in the Stonebreaker's Yard in Kilmainham Gaol.

In this photograph Mrs Pearse is wearing a brooch bearing the image of Patrick and William, which she wore for the rest of her life, carrying the memory of her two dead sons with her always. (*Courtesy of the Pearse Museum*)

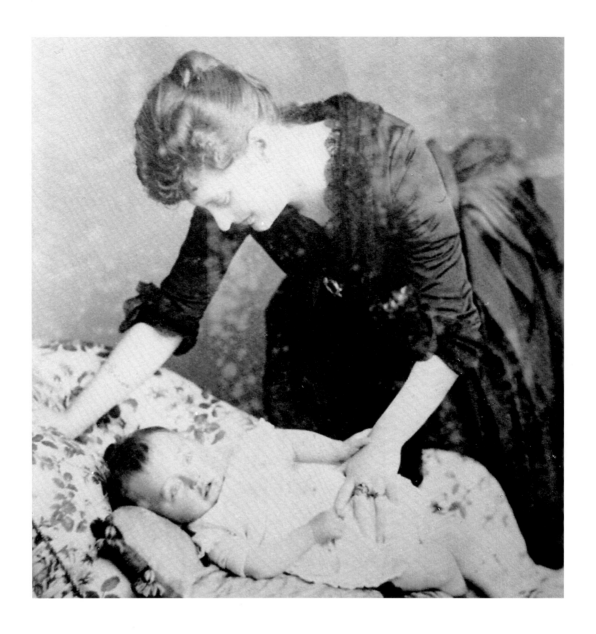

Countess Josephine Plunkett (*pictured with her daughter Mimi*) had three sons – Joseph, George and Jack – all of whom fought in the Easter Rising. Joseph had planned the strategy of the Rising and was a signatory of the Proclamation. He was engaged to Grace Gifford and they were due to be married on Easter Sunday, but this was postponed due to his involvement in the Rising. The couple were allowed to marry in Kilmainham Gaol in the Catholic chapel on 3 May, just a few hours before Joseph's execution. The only witnesses were the priest and two soldiers, and all they could say to each other were their wedding vows. Countess Plunkett and her husband were themselves arrested and the countess was held in Kilmainham Gaol. Upon her release a short time later she was sent by the authorities, along with her husband, to live in Oxford, England. They returned to Ireland following the general amnesty in 1917 and lived in Elgin Road, Ballsbridge. As a result of her sons' activities Countess Plunkett's home was constantly raided by the authorities, even though she herself was not an active participant in the War of Independence or the Civil War that followed. (*Courtesy of Honor Ó Brolchain*)

Maria Heuston (*right*), mother of Seán Heuston, who was a captain in the Irish Volunteers. He was in charge of a section of men in the Mendicity Institution, which fell under the command of Ned Daly. He was only meant to hold the building for a few hours to delay the British troops entering the city from nearby Kingsbridge (Heuston) Station. With less than twenty men he held the building for two days. Court-martialled, he was found guilty and sentenced to death.

The prelude to Seán's death provides an interesting insight into the impact that the imprisonment and death of men in the Rising could have on their families left behind. While awaiting execution, Seán was visited by his mother, his brother Michael, sister, aunt and Lil Heuston, his first cousin. Writing of their last meeting, Michael told how calm and prepared Seán was for what was to come, but his one worry was how his mother would cope after his death. He had been her financial support and in trying to ensure that she would be financially secure he wrote to his employers in the Great Southern and Western Railway asking them to forward to her any salary or pension that may be owed to him. Seán was executed in Kilmainham Gaol on 8 May; he was twenty-five years old. (*Courtesy of Kilmainham Gaol Archives, 21PO-1C45-27*)

Michael Mallin's widow Agnes and his five children, the youngest of whom never saw her father as she was born after his execution. Michael Mallin was a member of the ICA and was in charge of the St Stephen's Green/College of Surgeons garrison during the Rising. Following a court martial, he was executed on 8 May 1916. On 19 August 1916 Agnes gave birth to a baby girl whom she called Maura. For women like Agnes the events of Easter Week meant that they were not only mother, but also had to become father and breadwinner to support their families. The Irish National Aid Association was formed in May 1916 and was soon followed by the Prisoners' Dependants' Fund (later renamed the Irish Volunteer Dependants' Fund), set up by Kathleen Clarke. The aim of both was to help the relatives of those involved in the Rising who had died or were in prison. In August the organisations amalgamated to become the INAAVDF. Agnes received some money from the organisation but a more pressing worry for her was her children's education, as she could not afford to send them all to school. As a result Séamus and Seán had their fees for St Enda's paid by the INAAVDF, and her other children also received a grant for their education. Agnes continued to live in the home she had shared with her husband on Emmet Road, Inchicore, Dublin and during the War of Independence the house was regularly raided by crown forces. Under the Military Service Pensions Service Act of 1924 she was awarded 30 shillings a week. In that year she also moved to nearby Mount Brown and, having worked as a nurse before she got married, took a nursing job in the South Dublin Union and also became a school attendance officer. With the strain of the previous few years her health began to suffer and in that same year she contracted tuberculosis. Although she recovered, she never fully regained her health and died in 1932. She was fifty-seven. (*Courtesy of Kilmainham Gaol Archives, 17PC-1B52-07c*)

Alice Coyle (née Coffey) (*above right*) lived with her husband Henry in Leinster Street. Henry was a member of 'F' Company, 2nd Battalion, Dublin Brigade, Irish Volunteers and fought in the GPO during the Rising. They were married only five months at the time of the Easter Rising. He was killed in the evacuation of the GPO on Friday 28 April. Alice was pregnant at the time of his death. She had a healthy baby boy and named him Henry O'Rahilly Coyle. In less than a year Alice became a wife, a widow and a mother. In October 1920 Alice married Joseph Coughlan. Joseph was a member of the British Army who fought in the First World War, but upon his return to Ireland after the war became a member of the IRA and fought in the War of Independence. Alice had nine children in all, eight boys and one girl. She died in 1975 at the age of eighty-two. (*Courtesy of Patrick Coughlan*)

REPUBLICAN TRIPLETS.
Constance, Kathleen, and Grace. Born July 1917.

Daughters of Mr. and Mrs. Fullerton - Irish Citizen Army - with Countess Constance de Markievicz, Dr. Kathleen Lynn, and their father, representing Mrs. Grace Plunkett.

Both from the James Street area in Dublin, George and Elizabeth (Lizzie) Fullerton were married in 1904. By 1911 they had five children and lived in Bow Lane, near to the Royal Hospital, Kilmainham. George was a general labourer in the nearby Inchicore Railway Works, while Lizzie ran a shop where they lived. George took part in the 1913 Lockout and joined the ICA upon its inception, while Lizzie joined Cumann na mBan in 1914. During the Rising George fought under Michael Mallin in St Stephen's Green and the College of Surgeons. With a young family to care for, Lizzie did not take part in the fighting, but made her way into the city during the week to try to find out if George was okay. Unable to locate him she decided to return home but was wounded in the leg by a ricochet bullet on her way.

George survived the fighting but was arrested. On 3 May he was deported to Knutsford Prison in England and from there to Frongoch internment camp. Upon his release from Frongoch he returned to Ireland and settled back into family life. Soon he and Lizzie had the unexpected pleasure of not just one new arrival, but three. The Fullerton triplets, or 'Republican' triplets as they became known, were born in early July 1917. Through her membership with Cumann na mBan Lizzie had become close to many of the wives and dependants of those interned and imprisoned, and amongst those she was closest to were Countess Markievicz, Grace Gifford and Kathleen Lynn, who became the triplets' godmothers and after whom they were named. In the picture above two of the godmothers hold their goddaughters on the day of their christening: Grace Gifford is missing as she was attending the funeral of her sister Muriel, who had recently drowned. The Fullerton's joy was not to last as two of the triplets, Constance and Grace, died in a terrible accident when the pram that they were in toppled over, fatally injuring them when they were less than a year old. (*Courtesy of Phyllis Seale and Phyllis Foynes*)

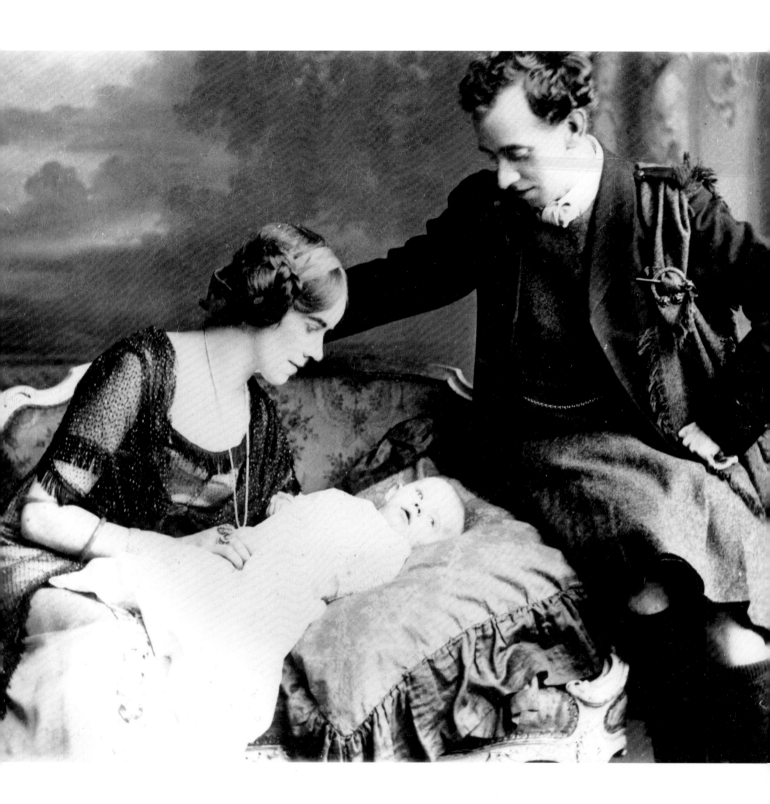

Muriel MacDonagh (née Gifford) was born in Dublin in 1884. Like her sisters, Muriel immersed herself in the cultural and nationalist revival. In 1911 she met her future husband Thomas MacDonagh when she and her sisters, Grace and Sidney 'John', went to Cullenswood House, Rathfarnham, where Patrick Pearse had set up his first school. They were accompanying Nora Dryhurst, who had been invited by Pearse to attend an open day there. MacDonagh was present. Muriel and Thomas soon became close. Despite their different religious backgrounds – Muriel was a Protestant and MacDonagh was a Catholic – they married on 3 January 1912. In November 1912 Muriel gave birth to their first child, a son, Donagh. Three years later she gave birth to a daughter, Barbara.

As a member of the Military Council of the IRB and a signatory of the Proclamation, Thomas MacDonagh would not live to see his children grow up. Easter Monday, 24 April, was the last time Muriel would ever see her husband as he left their home to take part in the Rising. During the Rising, as commandant of the 2nd Battalion, Dublin Brigade, Irish Volunteers, MacDonagh was in charge of the garrison in Jacob's Biscuit Factory, while Muriel made their home on Oakley Road, Ranelagh, available as a meeting place for the wives of those fighting.

Thomas MacDonagh was found guilty of taking part in an armed rebellion and the waging of war against the King at his court-martial, and was sentenced to death. Thomas MacDonagh was executed in Kilmainham Gaol on 3 May 1916. Upon hearing of her husband's wish to see her before his execution, Muriel desperately tried to get to Kilmainham. However, when she eventually arrived at the prison she was turned away by the soldiers and the couple were not given the chance to say goodbye to each other. Fr Aloysius of the Capuchin Order, Church Street, had to break the news of her husband's execution to her.

In the aftermath of his death, Muriel became a member of the committee of the INAAVDF. On 3 May 1917 the first anniversary of her husband's death, she converted to Catholicism. At this time the Dependants' Fund had rented a house in Skerries so that the families of those executed could have a holiday and help each other. Muriel, her children and her sister Grace took advantage of the offer of a holiday. On 9 July Muriel got into difficulty while swimming and drowned. Grace, Donagh and Barbara were on the beach collecting shells at the time. Seeing that her sister was in difficulty, Grace raised the alarm, but it was too late.

Muriel MacDonagh was buried with full military honours on 12 July 1917 in Glasnevin cemetery. She was thirty-three years old. (*Courtesy of Kilmainham Gaol Archives, 16PO-1A25-09*)

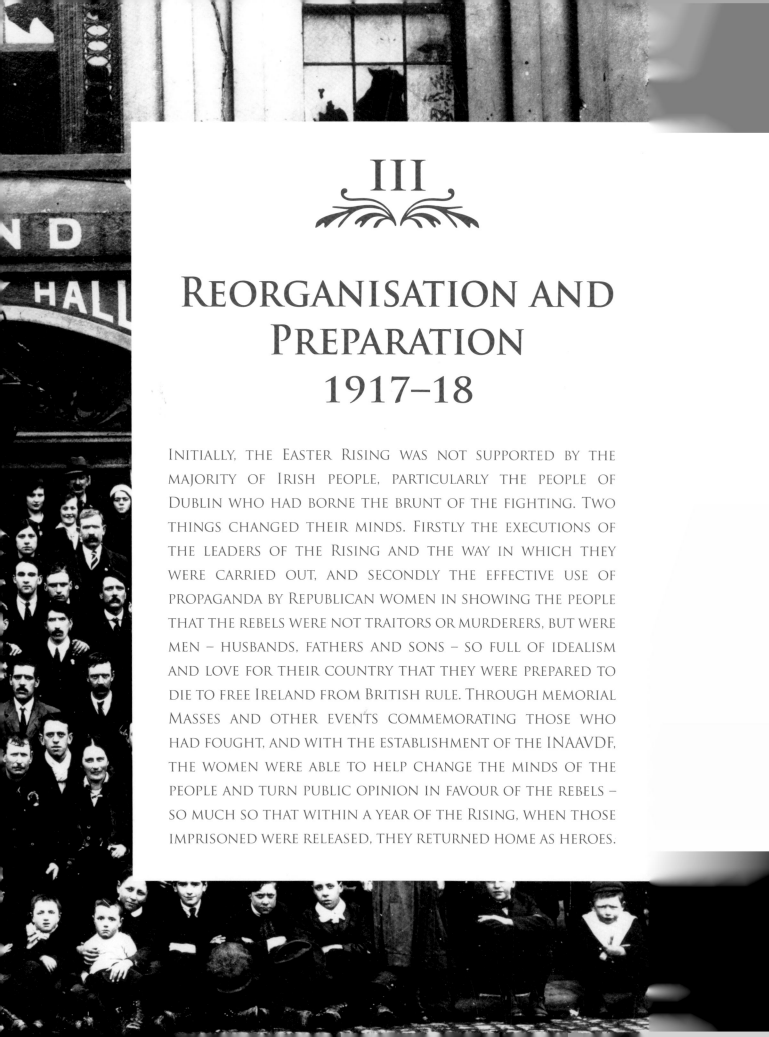

III

REORGANISATION AND PREPARATION
1917–18

INITIALLY, THE EASTER RISING WAS NOT SUPPORTED BY THE MAJORITY OF IRISH PEOPLE, PARTICULARLY THE PEOPLE OF DUBLIN WHO HAD BORNE THE BRUNT OF THE FIGHTING. TWO THINGS CHANGED THEIR MINDS. FIRSTLY THE EXECUTIONS OF THE LEADERS OF THE RISING AND THE WAY IN WHICH THEY WERE CARRIED OUT, AND SECONDLY THE EFFECTIVE USE OF PROPAGANDA BY REPUBLICAN WOMEN IN SHOWING THE PEOPLE THAT THE REBELS WERE NOT TRAITORS OR MURDERERS, BUT WERE MEN – HUSBANDS, FATHERS AND SONS – SO FULL OF IDEALISM AND LOVE FOR THEIR COUNTRY THAT THEY WERE PREPARED TO DIE TO FREE IRELAND FROM BRITISH RULE. THROUGH MEMORIAL MASSES AND OTHER EVENTS COMMEMORATING THOSE WHO HAD FOUGHT, AND WITH THE ESTABLISHMENT OF THE INAAVDF, THE WOMEN WERE ABLE TO HELP CHANGE THE MINDS OF THE PEOPLE AND TURN PUBLIC OPINION IN FAVOUR OF THE REBELS – SO MUCH SO THAT WITHIN A YEAR OF THE RISING, WHEN THOSE IMPRISONED WERE RELEASED, THEY RETURNED HOME AS HEROES.

Hannah Sheehy Skeffington (*shown here with her son Owen*) was married to Francis Sheehy Skeffington, who was arrested by Captain J. C. Bowen-Colthurst during the Rising, whilst attempting to organise a citizen's group to stop the looting that was taking place in the city, and was executed on the orders of Bowen-Colthurst. After the Rising Hannah undertook a lecture tour of America to highlight what had happened in Ireland. She raised $40,000 in America to put towards the Republican cause.

When Hannah attempted to return to Ireland the British government refused to grant permission for her to enter the country. Despite the ban Hannah managed to smuggle herself back to Ireland from Liverpool. As a result she was detained under the Defence of the Realm Act (DORA) and was imprisoned in Holloway Prison in England. She immediately went on hunger strike and was released. Upon her return to Ireland she gave the money she had raised in America to Michael Collins.

Hannah chose not to become a member of Cumann na mBan, as she felt that it was a subservient body to the Volunteers. She did, however, join Sinn Féin, becoming a member of its executive. During the War of Independence she was an organising secretary for Sinn Féin and was also a judge in the Republican Courts that were set up to undermine the official courts. She was a very effective propagandist for the nationalist movement.

In 1920 Hannah was elected to Dublin Corporation in the local elections held that year. She was involved with the White Cross upon its formation and was appointed to its executive. In 1922, along with Charlotte Despard and other women, she tried in vain to prevent civil war from breaking out. In November of that year Hannah, Linda Kearns and Kathleen Boland were sent by Éamon de Valera to America to raise money for the Republican cause.

When de Valera founded Fianna Fáil in 1926, Hannah joined the new party but her membership did not last long and she resigned as she did not agree with de Valera's decision to enter Dáil Éireann, which meant having to take the Oath of Allegiance. Hannah remained politically active as a Republican Socialist and in the 1930s she remained in contact with many of the IRA men who were still active at the time. She was very much an independent woman and earned her living from journalism and going on lecture tours. She opposed the Conditions of Employment Bill, introduced by the Fianna Fáil government in 1935. Hannah Sheehy Skeffington died in 1946. She was sixty-nine years old. (*Courtesy of the Library of Congress, LC-B2-4085-15*)

Kathleen Clarke (née Daly) was a founding member of Cumann na mBan and attached to the Central Branch of the organisation. Born in Limerick in 1878, she came from a very prominent Republican family. Her uncle, John Daly, had been imprisoned for his part in the Fenian dynamite campaign in England in the 1880s and it was through him that she met her future husband, Tom Clarke, a member of the IRB who had spent fifteen and a half years in prison in England. He was twenty years older than Kathleen, but despite this they fell in love. They emigrated to America and married in 1901. Tom was determined to return to Ireland to achieve his main goal in life – to see Ireland free from British rule. Kathleen relented and they returned in 1907. She was totally supportive of her husband's activities even though she knew it meant they would most likely never live a normal life together. She did not take an active part in the Easter Rising, although she was one of the few who knew of the plans, her role being to reorganise the Volunteers in the case of her husband's death. (*Courtesy of Kilmainham Gaol Archives, 18PO-1B53-15*)

Before the Rising Tom gave Kathleen a list of the names of men who would reorganise the movement if the Volunteer leadership did not survive. He also gave her gold which she used to set up the Prisoners' Dependants' Fund. Arrested under the 'German Plot', an alleged conspiracy between Germany and Irish Republicans to start an insurrection, she was imprisoned in England in 1918. A celebration was held in her honour upon her release later that year and was attended by members of Cumann na mBan. This photograph shows the event, with Kathleen seated under the flags, Harry Boland seated left and Michael Staines seated far right. Others in the photograph are Mary Harte, Dr Kathleen Lynn, Nancy Wyse Power (*seated front right*), Máire Deegan, Máire O'Neill, Chris Stafford, May Murray, L. McClean, Elizabeth Geraghty, Josie O'Keeffe, Maura O'Neill, Elish O'Connor, Lily Waters and Áine Ceannt. (*Courtesy of Kilmainham Gaol Archives, 19PO-1A33-29*)

Muriel Murphy came from a pro-British family and went to school in England. Returning to Cork she came to know the MacSwiney family and struck up a relationship with Terence, a member of the Cork Brigade of the Irish Volunteers. Muriel joined Cumann na mBan in 1915. After the round-up of Volunteers in Cork following the Rising, which included Terence, she went to Dublin and managed to get into Richmond Barracks where she saw both Terence and Tomás MacCurtain before they were deported. Following this, she helped with the National Aid Association and was asked by Seán O'Sullivan to go to England and visit the prisons to get information about the men being held there, which she agreed to do. Terence was released in December 1916 but was not allowed to return to Ireland. Despite this the couple became engaged and they married in June 1917. Richard Mulcahy was best man at their wedding.

The newlyweds returned to Cork but did not share a long life together. Terence was arrested in 1917, the same day that Muriel discovered she was pregnant – their daughter Máire was born in 1918. During and after her pregnancy Terence was imprisoned at least three times and was sent to Cork Gaol, Belfast Gaol, Dundalk Gaol and Lincoln Prison, England. In August 1920 Terence was arrested in Cork and sent to Brixton Prison, where he went on hunger strike. Muriel travelled to England and, with his sisters Mary and Annie and his two brothers, visited him in prison every day. Muriel pleaded with her husband to end the strike but he refused. Desperate, she contacted IRA headquarters and asked them to order him to come off the strike, but they would not intervene. Terence MacSwiney died on 25 October 1920 after seventy-four days on hunger strike. Muriel MacSwiney became a widow at the age of twenty-eight. (*Courtesy of Library of Congress, LC-F8-20510*)

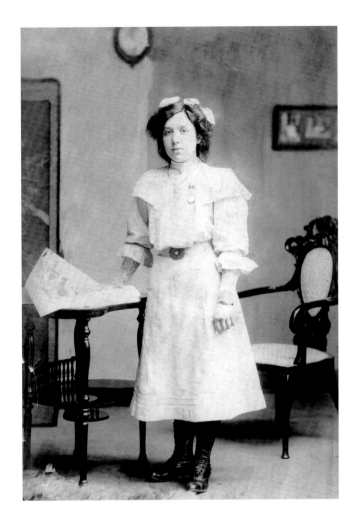

Nora McCarthy (née Quinn) was born in 1894 and lived in Scotland Street, Belfast. She was a member of the Belfast Cumann na mBan and it was through her Republican work that she met her future husband, Dan McCarthy. A member of the Volunteers, he was originally from Castleisland in Co. Kerry and had been arrested as part of the 'German Plot' in 1918 and was sent to Crumlin Road Gaol in Belfast along with fellow Kerrymen Austin Stack and Fionán Lynch. Demanding to be treated as political prisoners they staged a revolt in the prison, laying siege for a number of weeks until their demands for political status were met – they even managed to hoist a Tricolour above the gaol. They were eventually granted prisoner-of-war status. Nora, it seems, had some association with the prison guards and it is said that she would deliver a cargo of poitín (which she made herself) to the prison and in return would receive arms, ammunition and even prison guard uniforms, and also that she was responsible for getting Dan released from gaol, finding him a job as a tram and trolleybus driver in Belfast. The couple married and lived in Belfast, continuing their involvement in the Republican movement and were later involved in the National Graves Association. (*Courtesy of Adam O'Leary*)

Members of a committee formed in 1917 in Tipperary to commemorate the dead of 1916. This was just one example of how women helped to turn public opinion from one of anger against the Volunteers in 1916 into one of support. Through memorial concerts and picnics and other similar events they would have a platform from which to tell the people just what these men had fought and died for, and they were successful in their efforts. Front row (*left to right*): W. M. Whelan, B. Bourke, Dolly O'Keeffe, M. Power and B. Hickey; back row: M. H. O'Keeffe, J. McGuinness, D. Baldwin, J. Hickey, J. Babington and P. Power. (*Courtesy of Martin O'Dwyer*)

Winifred (Winnie) Carney was born in Bangor, Co. Down in 1887. She trained as a short-hand typist and, interested in learning the Irish language, she joined the Gaelic League in Belfast. She also became involved in the socialist movement and in 1912 became secretary to the Irish Textile Workers' Union. Through this she met James Connolly, who was living in Belfast at the time. She joined Cumann na mBan in Belfast in 1914 and over the next two years she remained in contact with James Connolly, who had moved to Dublin. Just before the Rising was due to begin, Connolly personally requested that Winnie come to Dublin. This she did and was to serve with Connolly as his secretary in the GPO throughout the whole of Easter Week. Arrested after the surrender, Winnie was imprisoned in Kilmainham Gaol, Mountjoy Prison and Aylesbury Prison in England. She was released in December 1916.

Winnie returned to Belfast upon her release and threw herself back into her political work, which was now more focused on the issues of workers' rights and social equality. She was elected as delegate representing the Belfast Branch at the National Convention of Cumann na mBan that was held in the autumn of 1917. She was also elected president of the Belfast Branch, Cumann na mBan. In the 1918 general election she stood for Sinn Féin in the Central/East Belfast Victoria Division, but was not elected.

During the War of Independence she worked for the INAAVDF in Belfast as secretary of the organisation. Like so many women her other role in the conflict was to shelter wanted IRA men from the authorities. She opposed the Treaty and during the Civil War she was arrested for 'carrying seditious documents' and was imprisoned in Armagh Gaol. An advocate of women's suffrage and the Republican cause, her true passion lay in the labour movement and she was a member of the Northern Ireland Labour Party. In 1928 she married George McBride – a surprising match as he was Protestant and a unionist, and had also been a member of the UVF. Winnie Carney died in 1943, aged sixty-six. She is buried in Milltown Cemetery in Belfast. (*Courtesy of Kilmainham Gaol Archives, 2012.0243*)

Members of the ICA outside the ruins of Liberty Hall, Easter 1917. Amongst those in the photograph is Winifred Carney, front row sitting beside the post to the left. Second to her left is Helena Molony and fifth to her left is Kathleen Lynn. All three women took part in the Rising. In May 1917 the veterans decided they would mark the anniversary of the death of James Connolly. On the instigation of Helena Molony a large scroll was placed across the windows of Liberty Hall reading 'James Connolly Murdered May 12th 1916'. The police were quick to take it down. Not willing to let the authorities get the better of them a new banner was quickly made. This time the women would do everything in their power to ensure the police would not remove this banner. Molony, with Rosie Hackett, Brigid Davis and Jinny Shanahan, went up to the roof of Liberty Hall. They barricaded the door to the roof and proudly unfurled their banner. These four women defied up to 400 policemen for four hours. Finally, after great effort, the police managed to break through the barricade and remove the banner. (*Courtesy of Military Archives, IE-MA-BMH-CD-119-3-5*)

Brigid Davis joined the ICA in 1915, where she assisted Dr Kathleen Lynn in teaching the women first aid in Liberty Hall. She was a member of the City Hall garrison during the Rising, under the command of her neighbour Seán Connolly and was second in command to Kathleen Lynn in the medical section. She was with Seán Connolly when he was shot by a British sniper. Following the surrender and arrest of the garrison she was taken to Ship Street Barracks. After a week she and her comrades were transferred to Richmond Barracks and then to Kilmainham Gaol. She was released with the main body of women on 8–9 May.

In 1918 the Spanish Flu epidemic was sweeping throughout the country with devastating effect. Davis and other ICA women assisted Dr Lynn in administering vaccines to the members of the ICA and their families, and nursed victims of the flu in their homes. That same year Dr Lynn, with Madeleine Ffrench-Mullen, Kathleen Clarke and others formed a committee to set up a hospital for infants. They acquired Charlemont House, which was almost derelict and, together with the women from the ICA, got the building in order. In 1919 St Ultan's Hospital for Sick Infants opened its doors, the first hospital of its kind in the country. In 1920, at Lynn's insistence, Brigid trained as a baby nurse and one year later was fully qualified.

Around this time Brigid joined Cumann na mBan. Throughout the War of Independence she tended to wounded Volunteers in secret locations until they could be transferred to hospitals friendly to the IRA. This is how she met her future husband, Paddy O'Duffy. A veteran of the Easter Rising, he had been interned in Frongoch. On his release he returned to 'E' Company, 2nd Battalion, Dublin Brigade. During the War of Independence he was wounded and Brigid was his nurse. They married in 1921. With the signing of the Treaty and the subsequent split in the Republican movement, O'Duffy took the pro-Treaty side, but Brigid took no part in the Civil War. (*Courtesy of Maureen Dawson*)

Members of Sinn Féin at the party's headquarters at No. 6 Harcourt Street, October 1918. Back row (*left to right*): Seán Milroy, Robert Brennan. Second row: Diarmuid O'Hegarty, Michael Nunan, Dan McCarthy, Michael Collins, Vera McDonnell, Desmond Fitzgerald, Anna Fitzsimmons, unidentified, Brian Fagan, Willie Murray. Front row: Joe Clarke, Barney Mellows, Jenny Mason, Ita Hegarty, Seamus Kavanagh, unidentified.

From its inception in 1905 Sinn Féin welcomed women into the party. In the years following the Rising the role of women in the party grew stronger and stronger. In the local elections of 1920 forty-three of its women members were elected to borough and urban councils and carried out their duties as councillors extremely well. The women were central to the organisation of Dáil Éireann and they worked in all of the various government departments as secretaries. But they were much more than secretaries and as the War of Independence escalated, more often than not they had to be constantly on the alert for impending raids on their offices by the authorities. They were not just responsible for the concealment of important documents but would have to ensure that there was always a secure line of escape from the premises for wanted men. This and many other tasks they fulfilled on a daily basis. (*Courtesy of Mercier Archive*)

In 1918 two events took place that Sinn Féin and the Republicans used to put their case to the people and undermine the government – the anti-conscription campaign and the general election. When the British government attempted to extend conscription to Ireland they were met with fierce resistance. In June, at the Women's Day Demonstration in Waterford, roughly 1,500 women paraded with banners bearing the slogan 'The Women of Waterford will not have Conscription'. In Tipperary 3,000 women paraded and signed the anti-conscription pledge. Conscription was not introduced to Ireland.

Cumann na mBan played a major role in the general election, which saw an overwhelming victory for Sinn Féin. Branches of Cumann na mBan all over the country campaigned for Sinn Féin candidates, distributing literature, escorting the elderly to the polling stations, manning the polling stations and even minding children so women could go and vote. On election day at the polling station on Drinan Street, Cork, they even set up a kitchen and fed the people. Their hard work paid off – of 105 seats Sinn Féin won 73. Countess Markievicz (*pictured*) was one of those elected, the first woman to be elected to the British parliament. Like her colleagues she refused to take her seat in Westminster. She was appointed Minister for Labour in the Dáil, the first woman in Western Europe to be appointed to a ministerial position. Over the next two and a half years she was arrested and imprisoned many times. The charges made against her included making seditious speeches and inciting the people to kill members of the police and military.

Markievicz opposed the Treaty and in the months before the Civil War was part of a delegation that went to America to raise financial support for the anti-Treaty Republicans. She lost her seat in Dáil Éireann in the general election in June 1922. (*Courtesy of Mercier Archive*)

A consequence of the 1918 general election result was that the authorities began to try to limit the rise of Republicanism by making even the smallest acts illegal, for example, waving a tricolour as this woman is doing, selling flags, collecting money without a permit and distributing literature. They also forbade the use of bicycles after a certain hour and even limited the distance a car could travel to twenty miles from its place of registration. Many women were arrested as a result, including May Conlon, Sarah Duggan, Kathleen Hayes, Myra Murphy, Nora O'Brien, Nellie Murphy and Nora Crowley. These women used their trials as platforms to gain support. Refusing to recognise the courts, they would often sing throughout the proceedings or chat amongst themselves, and they refused to pay the fines imposed on them. As a result they were more often than not sent to prison. (*Courtesy of Military Archives, IE-MA-BMH-CD-314*)

IV

THE WAR
OF INDEPENDENCE
1919–21

THE IRISH WAR OF INDEPENDENCE WAS NOTHING LIKE WHAT
HAD BEEN EXPERIENCED IN WARFARE BEFORE. THIS CONFLICT
WAS A NEW CONCEPT DEVISED BY THE IRA, WHO KNEW THAT
THEY WOULD NEVER DEFEAT THE BRITISH IN STAGED BAT-
TLES. THIS WAR WOULD BE FOUGHT TO THE IRA'S ADVANTAGE,
THROUGH AMBUSHES, QUICK ENGAGEMENTS AND, MOST IMPOR-
TANTLY, THROUGH THE USE OF INTELLIGENCE. THE WOMEN
PROVED TO BE THE REAL SECRET ARMY DURING THIS CONFLICT
AND WERE AN INTEGRAL PART OF THE REPUBLICAN INTELLI-
GENCE MACHINE. THEY CARRIED DISPATCHES, WEAPONS AND
AMMUNITION, AND BEFRIENDED SOLDIERS IN ORDER TO GAIN
VALUABLE INFORMATION ON THE CROWN FORCES. VERY OFTEN
THIS WORK WAS CARRIED OUT ALONE AND AT NIGHT. THE
WOMEN READILY TOOK ON THIS CHALLENGE AND SUCCEEDED
WHEN MOST WOULD HAVE FAILED. THEIR ACTIONS WERE JUST
AS CRUCIAL IN BRINGING ABOUT THE TRUCE BETWEEN BRITAIN
AND IRELAND IN JULY 1921 AS ALL OF THE AMBUSHES THAT
HAD TAKEN PLACE AROUND THE COUNTRY.

During the War of Independence Helena Molony continued to work at the Abbey Theatre while also carrying out her duties for the Republican movement. Molony was a courier for both Michael Collins and Liam Mellows. She was not a member of Cumann na mBan (although she was later made an honorary member) as it was felt by some members of the IRA, including Collins, that certain women, particularly those acting as intelligence agents, should not be affiliated to any organisation so as not to come to the attention of the authorities. Molony was, however, known to the authorities and her flat in Westmoreland Street was regularly raided. When she moved to nearby Bachelor's Walk, Cumann na mBan used her flat. She was also a district judge in the Republican Courts, a regular speaker at public meetings and worked for the INAAVDF.

Helena opposed the Treaty and during the Civil War she assisted the anti-Treaty IRA by sheltering wanted Republicans, tending to wounded men and concealing weapons, while her home on Bachelor's Walk was for a time used by the Republicans as their headquarters. She was never arrested.

A trade unionist at heart, Molony was organising secretary for the IWWU from 1929 until 1940 and was a member of the Dublin Trade Council. She was president of the Trade Union Congress in 1936. She also remained a committed Republican and was a member of the Urban District Council for Rathmines and Rathgar. She opposed the Conditions of Employment Bill, introduced by Fianna Fáil, which prohibited the employment of women in industry, and she became a member of Mná na hÉireann, a group set up to gain equality for women. Helena Molony died in 1967, aged eighty-four. (*Courtesy of Kilmainham Gaol Archives, 2011.0287*)

In October 1917 Áine Ceannt was co-opted onto the executive committee of Sinn Féin. Throughout the War of Independence 1919–21 she was a judge for the Sinn Féin Republican Courts and a district justice for Dublin South City, Rathmines and Rathgar. In December 1920, on the suggestion of Lord Mayor of Dublin Laurence O'Neill, the Irish White Cross was set up to help civilians who were suffering at the hands of the crown forces. Áine became involved in this organisation and from 1922 until 1947 she was secretary to the Irish White Cross Children's Relief Association. She was also a trustee of the INAAVDF.

During the War of Independence her house was raided by the military a number of times, but despite this she sheltered many wanted Republicans who were on the run from the authorities.

Like many of her comrades, especially the widows of the 1916 leaders, Áine rejected the Anglo-Irish Treaty. She was a founding member of the Irish Red Cross in 1939 and was honorary treasurer from that period until her resignation in 1947. Áine Ceannt died in 1954. She was seventy-four years old. (*Courtesy of Kilmainham Gaol Archives, 17PC-1B52-04*)

Cumann na mBan and other women were vital fund-raisers. Their efforts not only ensured that the IRA had money to purchase weapons but, very importantly, through concerts, weekly collections outside churches and other events, they raised huge sums for the INAAVDF to support the families of IRA men on the run, in prison or who had died. This work meant arrest for many women, but that did not deter them.

Members of the Éamonn Ceannt Branch of Cumann na mBan at a fund-raising event are shown here. Back row (*left to right*): unidentified, Mary Kate Nugent, Lil Harris, Molly Ronan, Bill Carr, Lil Coventry, Julia Cullen, May Graham and Rose Williamson; middle row: Maggie Whitty, Bridie Mullen, Sarah O'Mara, Kitty Harpur, May Harris, Nan Cullen, Lina O'Brien and Maisie Morrissey; front row: Mr Monigan, Tom Graham and Jim Byrne. (*Courtesy of Stephen Carey*)

Cumann na mBan members were trained in first aid and were always on call to assist wounded IRA men. They had to ensure that there were safe houses available where the men could be treated and at very short notice would often have to get the men away if the premises was about to be raided. They were often called on to go walking with wounded men who needed to exercise in the evening, pretending to be a courting couple so as not to bring any unwanted attention from the authorities. In the case of the Inghinidhe Branch, when they got notice of an impending ambush they would set up first aid stations near the proposed site ready to treat the wounded. In this photograph (*back row, left*) is Nora Byrne of the Éamonn Ceannt Branch. She and her sister Annie, who was also a member of Cumann na mBan, were from Mount Brown, Dublin. Note the first aid armbands worn by two of the women in the picture. (*Courtesy of Kilmainham Gaol Archives, 20PO-1B53-08b*)

The Irish War of Independence is generally credited with beginning on 21 January 1919, with the Soloheadbeg ambush in Tipperary instigated by Seán Treacy, Dan Breen and members of the 3rd Tipperary Brigade. During the war Tipperary was one of the most active areas in the country, but while the 3rd Tipperary Brigade was successful in many engagements against the crown forces, it would not have been nearly as effective without the help of the Tipperary Cumann na mBan and other women who gave it so much support, sheltering wanted IRA men and carrying out intelligence work.

In the photo above members of the 3rd Tipperary Brigade IRA and Cumann na mBan sit mixed together. Front row (*left to right*): Jack Reilly, Ed Hurley, Maurice McGrath, Cudge Lonergan, J. Power, Mary Glendon, Tom Coughlan and Jimmy Butler; middle row: Bridget Walsh, Brian Morrissey, Bob Sheehan, Johanna Butler, Mary Tobin, Paddy Baldwin and Bridgie Butler; back row: Julia Glendon, Jim (Cock) Norris, Ned Glendon, Hannah Walsh, Ned Butler, Jack Daly, Kitty Tobin, Jimmy Doherty, Bunny Foran, Tommy Kennedy and Frank Mullane. (*Courtesy of Martin O'Dwyer*)

Josephine O'Dwyer Grogan, captain of 'A' Company, Cashel Cumann na mBan. Prior to the War of Independence Josephine would regularly attend and speak at rallies which were held all over the country. These rallies were held for many reasons, including trying to get Republican prisoners released from prison, especially after the 'German Plot' arrests, and in the run-up to the general election in 1918. During the War of Independence, in her role as captain, Josephine had to ensure that there was a secure line of communication between the various Volunteer companies so that her members could safely carry dispatches. (*Courtesy of Martin O'Dwyer*)

Brigid (*left*) and Nora O'Keeffe, from Glenlough, Co. Tipperary, were members of Cumann na mBan attached to the 3rd Tipperary Brigade. Their brothers, Dan and Con, were members of that brigade. Dan fought in the Hammam Hotel in Dublin during the Civil War. Their sister's house in Kilshenane, Cashel, was a safe house for the IRA and was regularly used by the 'Big Four': Seán Treacy, Dan Breen, Seamus Robinson and Seán Hogan. Nora was in Dublin at the time of Seán Treacy's death in October 1920 and the job of identifying his remains in King George V Hospital fell to her. When she did this a British orderly gave her a lock of Treacy's hair and his ring.

Nora opposed the Treaty and during the Civil War she was imprisoned in both Cork and Kilmainham Gaols. She died in 1961, aged sixty-two. (*Courtesy of Martin O'Dwyer*)

Dolly Burke (*centre*) was from Ballinure, Co. Tipperary, and was a member of Cumann na mBan, attached to the 7th Battalion, 3rd Tipperary Brigade. Her brother Michael was a member of the IRA, as was her fiancé, Thomas Donovan, who was shot and killed by the crown forces in November 1920. Dolly was arrested in February 1921 and imprisoned in Cork Gaol. With the help of her comrades in the IRA and Cumann na mBan she managed to escape in September 1921. A man and two women went to the gaol requesting to see her. They were armed and by threatening the wardress they got the keys to the prison and were able to release Dolly. A painter who worked at the prison was later arrested for his involvement in the escape. Dolly was not recaptured. (*Courtesy of Martin O'Dwyer*)

Members of Cumann na mBan from Tipperary marching in the funeral procession of Volunteer Pierse McCan, 10 March 1919, Dualla, Co. Tipperary. McCan was a member of the Irish Volunteers in Tipperary and was also elected as a TD for East Tipperary in the 1918 general election despite the fact that he was in Gloucester Prison, England. While there he contracted the Spanish Flu and died on 6 March 1919. (*Courtesy of Martin O'Dwyer*)

Tommie Fahie of the 3rd Tipperary Brigade IRA with Mary Purcell, May Corbett and Helen Corbett, members of Cumann na mBan attached to that brigade. (*Courtesy of Martin O'Dwyer*)

Mary Ormonde (*standing, third left*) was a member of Waterford Cumann na mBan. This branch may not have appeared to have acted as a unit, like the other branches throughout the country, but that did not mean they contributed any less to the Republican movement. Waterford was a garrison town with a high proportion of military and police, so it suited the women in Waterford to be less visible than many of their counterparts. They were more likely to act individually when called upon by IRA officers for assistance. (*Courtesy of Waterford County Museum, EK 242*)

RIGHT

Anastasia Keating was a member of Cumann na mBan and she, like many of her colleagues, went on to marry a member of the IRA. This photograph was found in an autograph book that was kept in Ballykinlar camp during the War of Independence and most likely belonged to Volunteer Tommy Mooney, West Waterford Brigade, who was arrested and sent to Ballykinlar during the war. Anastasia and Tommy married in 1929. (*Courtesy of Waterford County Museum, UK 2694*)

After the Easter Rising Alice Cashel went to New York and Canada and met John Devoy, leader of Clan na Gael, the American wing of the IRB who had helped fund the Rising. Returning to Ireland in January 1917 she went to Cork and taught in St Ita's school which was run by Mary MacSwiney, while also continuing her work for Cumann na mBan. In February 1918 she was appointed as an organiser for Cumann na mBan and set up branches in Newry and Donegal, later helping in the campaign in Cavan for the general election. In 1919, while in Clifden trying to organise Cumann na mBan, she came to the attention of the authorities and had to go on the run, but she continued with her work organising branches in Mayo, Achill, Leitrim, Donegal and Fermanagh. Alice returned to Dublin at Easter 1919, as her health had begun to suffer because of this demanding work. She then went to Connemara and looked after her brother-in-law's oyster fishery. The police, believing she was using the fishery as a front to smuggle in weapons from America, raided the house she was living in and arrested her in April 1920. She was held in Galway Gaol for one week.

Alice was co-opted onto the District Council of Cashel, Co. Galway, and later Galway County Council, of which she was elected vice-chairman. She was also appointed as a parish justice to the Republican Courts in Connemara. She was again arrested in January 1921 and imprisoned in Galway Gaol for six months. She was released on 25 July, after which she went to Dublin where she worked for Erskine Childers in Sinn Féin's propaganda department. She wrote a pamphlet entitled 'Atrocities on Women' and as a Representative of Justice she worked as a liaison officer between the Irish Republican Police and the County Council. She was opposed to the Treaty and in February 1922 she resigned from her post as Representative of Justice on the Galway Committee and continued to work for the anti-Treaty forces until the end of the Civil War. (*Courtesy of Mark Humphrys*)

After the Rising ended, Leslie Price resumed her work with the Central Branch of Cumann na mBan, which saw her visiting wounded Volunteers, including Cathal Brugha, at Dublin Castle and Richmond Barracks. She was honorary treasurer of the INAAVDF and was elected onto the executive of Cumann na mBan. The authorities were aware of her activities so she gave up her teaching job and dedicated herself full-time to the Republican movement. She was appointed director of organisation of Cumann na mBan, a job which included travelling around the country setting up branches, but she was based mainly in Cork. She also helped Rory O'Connor plan the escape of Charlie Hurley, O/C of the 3rd West Cork Brigade, from Maryborough Prison in Portlaoise.

Communication between the country brigades and headquarters in Dublin was vital and it fell to Cumann na mBan to put in place a system of communication between them. Leslie Price was responsible for keeping a complete line of communication open from Dublin to Cork. Through her work with the Cork Brigade she and Charlie Hurley became close and were soon engaged. However, Hurley was killed on 19 March 1921 on the eve of the Crossbarry ambush, which was carried out under the command of his close friend Tom Barry, O/C West Cork flying column. After Charlie's death, Leslie and Tom became close and were married on 22 August 1921 in Vaughan's Hotel, Dublin. The wedding, as can be seen from this photograph, with Tom and Leslie flanking Éamon de Valera, was attended by a who's who of the Republican movement. Unfortunately, less than a year later many of these men would be fighting on opposite sides in the Civil War and would fall at the hands of their former friends.

Leslie and Tom opposed the Treaty and were both active in the Civil War. Tom was arrested a number of times and Leslie was active in the Four Courts, Barry's Hotel, Tara Hall and the Hammam Hotel, preparing first aid and cooking for the anti-Treaty forces in those garrisons. After Tom's arrest and the end of the fighting in Dublin, Leslie went to Kilkenny, where she was arrested but soon released. Back in Dublin she helped plan an attempted escape from Mountjoy Prison and continued to assist the anti-Treaty forces until the ceasefire. (*Courtesy of Mercier Archive*)

Eilís Ní Riain, shown here in Cumann na mBan uniform, was born in Longford, but moved to Dublin when she was quite young. She was a member of the Keating Branch of the Gaelic League and in August 1915, inspired by the Republican fervour of the funeral of Jeremiah O'Donovan Rossa, she joined the Central Branch of Cumann na mBan. During the Easter Rising she served first with the garrison in Reis's Chambers opposite the GPO carrying dispatches and was later sent to the garrison in the Four Courts where she assisted in first-aid duties and feeding the men at the various barricades throughout the area. Her sister Áine, also a member of Cumann na mBan, served in the GPO.

Eilís avoided arrest after the surrender and helped collect and distribute money for the INAAVDF. She and Leslie Price set up a branch of Cumann na mBan in Drumcondra, of which she was treasurer, but they both retained membership of the Central Branch. At the Central Branch's annual meeting in 1917 Eilís was elected vice-president. She took part in the funerals of Thomas Ashe in 1917 and Richard Coleman the following year, while also helping to campaign in Longford for the general election as well as the anti-conscription campaign in 1918. She replaced Leslie Price as captain of the branch when Leslie resigned to take up work as an organiser for Cumann na mBan in Munster, and was also elected vice-commandant of the Dublin District Council, Cumann na mBan.

In 1920 she was appointed to the Department of Finance and later to the Department of Labour in the new Dáil Éireann. These appointments brought her to the attention of the authorities, and she was forced to move out of her home and live under a false name, 'Mrs Talbot'. With Lily O'Brennan, she carried out intelligence work for the IRA, while also collecting wounded IRA men from hospitals that were unsafe. In October 1920 she was elected to the executive of Cumann na mBan, but both she and Lily O'Brennan resigned from the executive in 1921 due to their commitments to the INAAVDF and their work assisting wounded IRA men. Eilís later married Seán O'Connell, who had been a member of the IRA. Eilís died in 1981, aged eighty-seven. (*Courtesy of Military Archives, BMH CD 202.1*)

May Gibney was born in Dublin in 1894. She was a member of the Central Branch of Cumann na mBan and during the Easter Rising she served in the GPO. She avoided arrest after the surrender and continued to be active in the following years as an organiser for Cumann na mBan. During the War of Independence she was sent to Carlow to help set up branches of the organisation there. She also became engaged to Dick McKee, O/C Dublin Brigade. McKee was murdered by crown forces along with Peadar Clancy, vice-O/C Dublin Brigade, and Conor Clune, on 'Bloody Sunday', 21 November 1920, in Dublin Castle in reprisal for the assassinations carried out by the Squad earlier that morning. (*Courtesy of Kilmainham Gaol Archives, 20PC-1A22-16a*)

Margaret Craven (née Farrell) (*left*) and Agnes Brady (née Craven) (*right*) were childhood friends from Dublin's south inner city. Agnes was born in Clanbrassil Street in 1900 and Margaret was born in nearby Patrick Street in 1901. They were both members of Cumann na mBan and Margaret was attached to the College of Surgeons garrison during the Rising.

Both women took part in the War of Independence carrying dispatches, ammunition and weapons, including hand grenades, for the IRA. As the war escalated, the authorities became increasingly suspicious of women, who took greater risks in carrying out their work. One inventive but highly dangerous way women, including Agnes and Margaret, concealed the weapons was in their underwear.

Neither Agnes nor Margaret was arrested during the revolution, after which they settled into domestic life. Already friends, they became even closer when Margaret married Agnes' brother Mick in 1925. Agnes married Joe Brady in 1926. He had fought in the Easter Rising, War of Independence and was a member of the National Army during the Civil War. They had five children. Agnes Brady died in 1963, aged sixty-three. Margaret Craven died in 1993. She was ninety-two years old. (*Courtesy of Kilmainham Gaol Archives, 17PC-1B52-29*)

This photo shows the women of the Daly family: (*front row left to right*) Laura, Nora and Carrie; (*back row left to right*) Madge, Mrs Catherine Daly and Agnes (Úna). The Dalys were a strong Republican family from Limerick. Although the more famous of the sisters, Kathleen, did not actively participate in the Easter Rising, Nora Daly did take part, bringing verbal messages from Dublin to Cork. Their brother, Ned, was executed for his part in the Easter Rising.

As a result of their family connections, the Dalys were well known to the British authorities and during the War of Independence their family home and business in Limerick were raided regularly by the military and RIC. In one particular raid in October 1920 both Úna and Carrie were physically attacked by the crown forces. They had guns put to their faces and Úna was dragged by her hair from the house. The attackers then cut her hair and her hand was slashed with a razor. The attack was so savage that she nearly died. (*Courtesy of Kilmainham Gaol Archives, 17PC-1B52-05*)

Máirín Cregan was born in Killorglin, Co. Kerry, in 1891 and was encouraged by her mother to learn the Irish language. She became a teacher and taught in Kilkenny from 1911 until 1914 and there she met Margaret Browne, who became her lifelong friend and fellow activist. Following this Máirín moved to Dublin to study music and to pay for her lessons she taught at St Louis' High School in Rathmines. She joined the Gaelic League, which met in Kit Ryan's house, and there she met her future husband, Kit's younger brother Jim, who was studying medicine.

As she became more involved in politics, she was asked to sing at Volunteer concerts held in Parnell Square to raise funds for the Volunteers. She knew Seán MacDiarmada, who sent her to Tralee with weapons and ammunition for the local Volunteers before the Rising. She didn't know what she was carrying but successfully delivered her cargo, transporting it in her violin case. She was unable to get back to Dublin for the Rising and when she eventually did return she found that many of her close friends were either in prison or had been executed.

As a result of her Republican activities she lost her job, but managed to find work teaching in Ballyshannon and Portstewart. She continued to work for the Republican movement and helped campaign for Sinn Féin in the general election. She and Jim married in 1919 and she went to Wexford town where Jim had a general practice and was elected as TD to South Wexford in 1918.

While in Wexford Máirín joined the local Cumann na mBan. As the War of Independence escalated it became dangerous for Jim to stay at home and she was left alone at night and feared the house being raided, which did happen on occasion. Jim was arrested in December 1920 and transferred to Waterford Gaol in 1921.

After an IRA ambush in Wexford, six prominent Republicans, including Máirín, were ordered to post a proclamation of martial law in the windows of their homes. Máirín refused to comply and was imprisoned in Waterford Gaol for ten days, despite the fact that she had an eight-month-old baby, whom she was prohibited from seeing while incarcerated. She was tried by field court martial and given seven days to pay a £50 fine. Máirín refused to recognise the court and refused to pay the fine. She was threatened with three months' imprisonment with hard labour, but still she refused to pay. The arrest and imprisonment of a young mother had drawn so much attention that questions relating to the incident had been raised in the House of Commons. This was not the kind of publicity the British government needed and when she returned to the prison to serve her sentence the authorities would not let her in. Although she was now a free woman, it was not safe for Máirín to stay in Wexford and she went on the run, moving to her father-in-law's house in Dublin. There she worked for Robert Brennan in the Dáil's Department of Foreign Affairs which involved her travelling to London to the Republican envoy, Art O'Brien, and to Seán T. O'Kelly in Paris.

Máirín and her husband Jim took the anti-Treaty side during the Civil War. Jim was imprisoned again, during which time he took part in the hunger strike in late 1923. They had two young children, Nuala and Seamus (*pictured above with their mother*). Jim was eventually released and the couple finally settled into normal family life, nearly six years after they were married, in Delgany, Co. Wicklow. Jim was a founding member of Fianna Fáil and served in government from 1932 until his retirement in 1965. In the meantime Máirín began a successful career as an author of books for both young and adult audiences, as well as a becoming a playwright. Drawing on her own experiences during the Civil War she wrote a play about the hunger strike of 1923 and the effect it had on the women whose husbands were involved. Máirín died in 1975. She was eighty-four years old. (*Courtesy of Jim Ryan*)

Daughter of Edward O'Brien, a Catholic, and Elizabeth Case, a Protestant, Mary Elizabeth O'Brien changed her name to Máirín in the early years of the revolution. The boys in the family were raised Catholic, the girls were raised in the Church of Ireland faith. This became a problem when Máirín began a relationship with Eamon Martin, who lived in the street behind her. They became sweethearts when they were teenagers and Eamon's parents, devout Catholics, did not approve of their relationship. Eamon was involved with Na Fianna Éireann and the Irish Volunteers and was seriously wounded when fighting in the Easter Rising. He went to America for eight months to aid his recovery and when he returned to Ireland he became chief of staff of Na Fianna. He and Máirín were married in 1918.

Máirín joined Cumann na mBan and during the War of Independence assisted her husband with Na Fianna, helping with administration and planning from a tailor's shop that Eamon ran on Arran Quay, Dublin. This building was used as a meeting hall for Na Fianna as well as a safe house. Máirín often brought messages and weapons to Na Fianna and the Volunteers, and she had her own network of women to help her carry out this work.

As a result of their role in the revolution, their early years of married life were not easy. Their first child, Roisin, was born in March 1920, but Eamon had to go abroad as he was a wanted man. Their second child, Eileen, was born in August 1921 during the Truce and Máirín hoped that now they could have a normal life together. But Eamon took the anti-Treaty side during the Civil War and was arrested and held in Mountjoy Prison. When he was eventually released they settled into married life with their young family. Máirín Martin died in 1945, at the age of fifty. Eamon died in 1971. This couple was just one of many who were devoted to each other and devoted to their country and both helped make a difference in the cause of independence. (*Courtesy of Eamon Murphy*)

Jennie Clery, born in 1892, was from Sandycove, Dublin. Despite coming from a pro-British family, she and her brother, Fr Bernard Clery, were staunch nationalists. She was a member of Cumann na mBan and was always on hand to deliver weapons to the Volunteers. She even gave them her father's guns, leaving the downstairs window of their house unlocked so the guns could be taken. She was often armed herself, but managed to avoid being searched by the troops by telling them that she had two brothers fighting in the British Army in the war: Lieutenant D. R. Clery and William J. Clery were members of the 6th Royal Dublin Fusiliers.

Jennie was with a group of nationalist supporters at Dun Laoghaire to see de Valera and his fellow inmates return from prison in 1917. Although she did not smoke herself she had some cigarettes with her to give to them.

She was the first lady bank official in the Munster and Leinster Bank and worked in their O'Connell Street Branch. Through her position there, during the War of Independence she was able to receive and pass messages to ordinary IRA men and the intelligence units, as they would pretend to be lodging money in the bank and give her the information which she would deliver after work. Sometimes the messages she received would be from an IRA man on the run who wanted to contact his wife or mother. It was because of women like Jennie that the intelligence war was such a success; they were an invisible army who were more than capable of doing whatever was asked of them. Jennie Clery died in 1978 at the age of eighty-six. (*Courtesy of Anne Regan*)

Eileen Bell was born in 1903 in Dublin and was the eldest of ten children. Her interest in Irish affairs came from her parents: her mother was from a Republican family and her grandfather was a Fenian who had been imprisoned in Mountjoy for his Republican activities. Her mother helped in the soup kitchens during the Lockout and this environment undoubtedly led to Eileen becoming involved in the nationalist movement. She joined the Drumcondra Branch of Cumann na mBan in 1920 when she was only seventeen years old.

Eileen was working as a tie-maker in Dublin when she joined Cumann na mBan. One of her many tasks during the War of Independence was to conceal and hold weapons for the IRA in her family home and although it was raided many times by British forces, nothing was ever found. During one raid she pretended to be asleep and was not disturbed, so the raiders left empty-handed – Eileen had 'slept' with the gun under her pillow.

Eileen opposed the Treaty and during the fighting in Dublin was in Barry's Hotel, Gardiner's Row, the headquarters of Oscar Traynor's anti-Treaty command before he moved to 'The Block' on O'Connell Street. (*Courtesy of Aileen Murray and Anne May*)

Dolly Lawlor's family home and shop were used as arms dumps by the Volunteers and her brothers and father would regularly get weapons from the soldiers at the Royal (now Collins) Barracks. During the Rising Dolly brought weapons and ammunition from home to the Volunteers stationed in North Brunswick Street, Blackhall Place and the Four Courts, as well as carrying dispatches between the Courts and the Mendicity Institution across the River Liffey. After the Rising she continued with her work in Cumann na mBan, helping with the general election and raising money for the Volunteers' Arms Fund. Throughout the War of Independence she was involved in preparing and delivering parcels to IRA men in prison. Her family home in Manor Street was well known to the authorities. On 16 October 1920 her father Peter was shot and killed by Major Jocelyn Lee Hardy, intelligence officer attached to the Auxiliaries in Dublin Castle, when a patrol of Auxiliaries went to the house looking for Dolly's brothers who were members of the IRA. Dolly had only been married to Larry Lawlor two weeks before her father's murder. A friend of her brothers, Larry was also in the IRA and had fought in 1916. They went on to have five children. (*Courtesy of Bernadine and Audrey Flanagan*)

Members of Sinn Féin at their Ard-Fheis outside Rathmines Town Hall, Dublin, 17 November 1925. *Left to right*: C. Daly, D. Baruls, P. G. Brennan, Éamon de Valera, Dulcibella Barton, Countess Markievicz and Éamonn Donnelly.

Dulcibella Barton was the sister of Robert Barton. Although initially not a supporter of the nationalist movement, her opinion changed after the Easter Rising. Her brother Robert was an important influence on Dulcibella. He had been a member of the British Army and served in Dublin during the Rising. He witnessed the treatment of many of the leaders in Richmond Barracks, which led him to support the Republican movement. In 1917 Dulcibella set up a Sinn Féin Club in Laragh, Co. Wicklow. During the War of Independence her home in Co. Wicklow was used to shelter IRA men on the run and Dulcibella often had to act as a guide for country Volunteers who were not familiar with the journey to Dublin. She also nursed wounded IRA men. She opposed the Treaty and during the Civil War she again sheltered wanted IRA men, including her cousin Erskine Childers who was arrested near her home in November 1922. (*Courtesy of Kilmainham Gaol Archives, 21PO-1A51-22*)

Rose O'Connor (née Fitzsimons) married her husband Jack in 1917 when he was on leave from the British Army during the First World War. Rose had witnessed first-hand the events of the Easter Rising, as she lived in North Earl Street at the time, but was not involved in the events of that week. However, they obviously had a serious impact on Rose, who despite being a young wife and just starting her married life, became a member of Cumann na mBan. She devoted her time to rearing her young family, while contributing to the revolutionary movement by collecting and distributing the money raised by Cumann na mBan for the INAAVDF, fully supported by her husband Jack, who was demobilised at the end of the war. Rose took the pro-Treaty side during the Civil War. In these photographs we see Rose with her daughter May born in 1919, and with Jack and her children (*left to right*) Chrissie, May and Phillip. (*Courtesy of Joan and Siobhan Treacy*)

Sr Eileen O'Dwyer, Rossmore, Cashel Convent, was a member of Cumann na mBan while also following her vocation as a nun. The order was aware of her Republican activities but did not prevent her from contributing to the revolutionary movement. Throughout the War of Independence various orders of priests and nuns were of great help and support to the IRA, despite the fact that it could and did bring the unwanted attention of the authorities. Certainly as the war progressed not even convents or priests' houses were immune from raids by the crown forces. (*Courtesy of Martin O'Dwyer*)

Sheila Fleming was from The Swan in Co. Laois and, along with her older brothers Patrick and Eamon, was involved in the independence movement. Sheila was a member of 'A' Company, The Swan Branch, Cumann na mBan, which during the War of Independence was attached to the North Kilkenny Brigade IRA. She was an organiser for Cumann na mBan in the south-east area of Co. Laois and was responsible for organising branches of Cumann na mBan in the townlands of The Swan and Wolfhill, to name a few. During the War of Independence she gathered intelligence for the local IRA units which entailed observing the movements of the local RIC. (*Courtesy of Jim Fleming*)

Members of Cumann na mBan at a vigil outside Mountjoy Prison. Through vigils like the one seen here, Cumann na mBan generated international media attention, helping to highlight what was happening in Ireland. These scenes were common throughout Dublin, Cork and other counties, where day after day the women would arrive at gaols, praying for the safety of those imprisoned, particularly during the hunger strikes of April 1920, and later during the executions of Kevin Barry and his comrades in Mountjoy Prison in 1920 and 1921. (*Courtesy of the National Library of Ireland, HOG 164*)

After Count George Noble Plunkett won his seat for Roscommon in the 1918 general election, Brighid O'Mullane from Co. Sligo was asked to help organise a banquet in his honour to be held in Sligo. His wife, Countess Plunkett, was staying at her home and told Brighid all about Cumann na mBan and suggested that she should set up a branch in Sligo. This she did and became honorary secretary of the branch. She was so efficient in her work that she was appointed an official organiser for Cumann na mBan, tasked with establishing branches throughout the country. She successfully set up nine branches.

Her job as an organiser was a lonely one and she had to travel long distances on a push bike. As a result of this gruelling work her health suffered and her weight plummeted to six and a half stone, but she only received medical help after the Truce.

She also enforced the boycott of the RIC and in October 1919 she was arrested and charged with 'inciting the people to murder the police'. Sentenced to two months' hard labour, she spent most of her imprisonment in solitary confinement in Sligo Gaol. On her release she returned to her work, which was becoming increasingly dangerous due to the arrival of the Black and Tans and Auxiliaries, whom she had more than one close encounter with. She also assisted local IRA units in their attacks against the authorities.

In 1920 she was sent to Belfast and set up branches of Cumann na mBan in Downpatrick and Portglenone. In fact she was so successful in her work that the IRA believed she was a spy and planned to assassinate her in Naas. Luckily she found out about this plan in advance and was able to prove that she was not a spy. However, there was a spy in the organisation and O'Mullane and Máire Comerford discovered who she was and set a trap for her. They pretended to organise for her to meet with the GHQ staff in Dublin, but instead she was met by O'Mullane and Comerford and arrested, whereupon it was discovered she was armed. The spy was tried, found guilty and ordered to leave the country.

O'Mullane opposed the Treaty and became the anti-Treaty Cumann na mBan's director of propaganda. She was in Sligo when the Civil War began, but made her way to Dublin, where she carried dispatches for the anti-Treaty IRA as well as weapons. She was a member of the guard of honour at the funeral of Cathal Brugha. She was arrested in November 1922 and taken to Mountjoy Prison, and was there during the executions of Rory O'Connor, Liam Mellows, Richard Barrett and Joe McKelvey. She was transferred to Kilmainham in 1923 and was appointed O/C of the prisoners in 'A' Wing. She organised a hunger strike in protest at the way the women were being treated and was involved in the riot that resulted from the women being transferred from Kilmainham to the NDU.

She remained a committed Republican all her life and was a founding member of the Irish Red Cross. Brighid died in 1967, aged seventy-four. (*Courtesy of the National Museum of Ireland*)

Above left: Annie Coyne (*left*) and Hanora (Nora) Traynor.
Above right: Nora Traynor, her brother Paddy and their mother Maria.

Hanora (Nora) Traynor was born in Dublin in 1893 and was the youngest in a family of six children. She attended St Agatha's Sisters of Charity girls' school in North William Street where she met Annie Coyne. The two became lifelong friends. Nora then attended Carysfort College, Blackrock, and trained to be a teacher. Three of her older brothers, Oscar, Paddy and Peter, all joined the 2nd Battalion, Dublin Brigade, Irish Volunteers in 1914. Influenced by her brothers' decision Nora, with her friend Annie, joined the Fairview Branch of Cumann na mBan and both were present at the funeral of O'Donovan Rossa in Glasnevin Cemetery in August 1915. Neither Nora nor Annie took part in the Easter Rising. Nora was asked by her brothers not to get involved so there would be someone left to look after their elderly mother.

After the Rising her brothers were imprisoned in England. Nora and Annie travelled over to visit them and bring them news from home and some home comforts. When Oscar returned home he and Annie began dating, while Nora began to date Oscar's friend and fellow Volunteer Peter Gilligan. Both couples were married in 1918. After her marriage Annie did not play an active part in the War of Independence but was no doubt a great support to her husband, who in 1920 became O/C of the Dublin Brigade IRA. This undoubtedly was a source of great stress for Annie, who would have worried about the safety of her husband. Nora was in a similar position but had the added stress of not just worrying about her husband but also her brothers' safety. During the War of Independence, Nora lived with her mother in Bayview Avenue. The house was regularly used as an arms dump and a safe house by the IRA. On 21 November 1920, now known as 'Bloody Sunday', Nora hid a rifle under the floorboards in her home and when it was safe to do so she managed to get the gun to another location. Both Nora and Annie opposed the Treaty. Although not taking an active part in the Civil War themselves, their husbands were active on the anti-Treaty side. Nora died in 1979. She was eighty-six years old. (*Courtesy of Donal Gilligan*)

With the arrival of the Black and Tans in March 1920 and the Auxiliaries in August that year, the War of Independence entered a new phase of terror and violence. Since 1918 there had been a boycott of the RIC in place, instigated by Sinn Féin, in which members of the public, and especially young women, were encouraged not to have any contact with the force. This was extended to the Tans and Auxiliaries. This stricture was not always heeded, as can be seen in this photograph. Some young women associated freely with them and were subjected to very severe punishment by the Republicans. In many cases the punishment was carried out by the women in whose locality they lived. The most common form of punishment was to have their hair cut and in some instances they were tarred and feathered. (*Courtesy of Military Archives, Fintan Murphy Collection, IE-MA-BMH-CD-227-35*)

Cumann na mBan, together with Sinn Féin, the Volunteers and other bodies were proscribed by the government, making it harder for them to meet. This did little to deter Cumann na mBan, who successfully held their annual convention in October 1920. Originally to be held in the Mansion House, the premises were put under constant watch by the authorities, so the priests from Whitefriar Street church offered the women a room at the back of the church in which to hold their meeting. They accepted, and entered the church in twos and threes as if going to Mass. The authorities never suspected a thing. This convention was literally a who's who of Cumann na mBan and no doubt the authorities would have liked to have had all of them in custody. This photograph taken at the convention shows (*group facing camera, left to right*): Mabel Fitzgerald, Mary MacSwiney, Louise Gavan Duffy, Miss O'Rahilly, Mrs Áine O'Rahilly, Máire O'Reilly, Mrs Pearse, Countess Markievicz, Kathleen Clarke, Áine Ceannt, Nancy Wyse Power, Madge Daly, Elizabeth Bloxam, Jenny Wyse Power, Fanny Sullivan, Lily O'Brennan. (*Courtesy of Military Archives, BMH CD 216.3*)

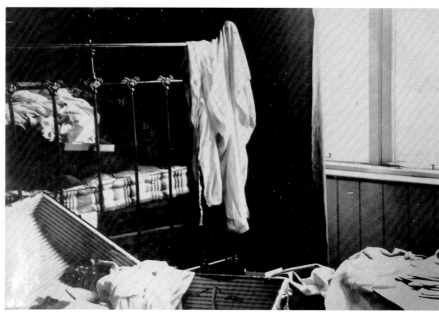

Raids on the houses of suspected or known Republicans were a common occurrence as the war progressed and because of this the women working in the various Sinn Féin offices around the city had to be alert, making sure there was a plan of escape for IRA men and others in the movement. Through their quick thinking they ensured the safety of many wanted men, including Michael Collins, and often had to endure the full force of the Auxiliaries' intimidation, but never relented or showed any sign of weakness; to them it was just part of their work. These images show the aftermath of a raid on 21 Dawson Street by 'F' Company, Auxiliaries, 31 December 1920. (*Courtesy of Military Archives, BMH CD 266-7-2-(a), CD 266-7-(c), CD 266-7-(d)*)

Kathleen Davin was from Rathsallagh, Rosegreen, Co. Tipperary. The Davins were a staunchly Republican family. Her brother Jerome was commandant of the 1st Battalion, 3rd Tipperary Brigade and Kathleen and her sister Eily were members of Cumann na mBan. Their house in Rathsallagh was always open to the IRA and was headquarters for the battalion and the brigade. They had a dugout constructed on their land which Volunteers on the run would use as sleeping quarters, while the brigade staff used it to hold meetings and plan operations. Kathleen later became a nun. (*Courtesy of Kilmainham Gaol Archives, 19PO-1A32-19*)

This picture shows the Brady family from Belfast. Front row (*left to right*): Mary Ann Brady and James Brady Senior; middle row: Mary, Francis, Beatrice and Kay Brady; back row: Jim Brady.

James Brady worked his way up through the linen industry and eventually became co-director of Nicholson/ Templeton in Belfast, the only Catholic to do so. He and his wife Mary Ann (Minnie) had six children, two boys and four girls: only Gerard is missing from the picture. They ensured that their daughters attended university, which they did in Belfast, Dublin, Germany and Brussels. Mary Ann, especially, wanted her daughters to be financially independent.

James was a nationalist who was involved in the White Cross and the Belfast Boycott, which was introduced in September 1920 in response to anti-Catholic pogroms that had begun in July. It was proposed that all goods coming from Belfast be boycotted and committees were set up all over the country to ensure the boycott was enforced. People were told to remove their savings from the Ulster Bank, a request supported by many businessmen like James. Any firm or business that ignored the boycott was liable to be boycotted itself. James Brady greatly influenced his children with his political beliefs – all were committed Republicans and he fully supported them in their activities.

Francis (Frank) Brady was born in 1892 and was educated in the St Louis Convent, Monaghan. She studied the cello in Brussels and in 1916 she began working in the censorship section of the British War Office in London.

Soon after this she joined the London Branch of Cumann na mBan. Michael Collins was aware of her work and she was contacted to work as an intelligence agent for him, passing on any information that might be useful. Frank returned to Belfast in 1919 and attended Queen's University. In 1920 she moved to Dublin and became involved in the Belfast Boycott campaign, which brought her all over the country. At this time she was also working as a courier for members of Dáil Éireann. On 3 June 1921 she was arrested at her sister Kay's house in Lower Leeson Street, which was being used at the time as a base of operations for the boycott. Following a court martial, Frank was sentenced to two years in Mountjoy Prison. She and a number of the other female political prisoners went on hunger strike to protest their treatment there. Frank was released in December 1921. She opposed the Treaty and worked as a courier for the anti-Treaty IRA. In 1924 she met Andy Cooney, quartermaster-general of the anti-Treaty IRA, and they married in September 1929 and had one son, Seán, who was born in 1931. Frank Brady died in 1977, aged eighty-five.

Mary (May) Brady was also educated in the St Louis Convent, Monaghan, and went to Queen's University, Belfast, where she studied languages. May joined Cumann na mBan after the Easter Rising and later worked on the Belfast Boycott. She also opposed the Treaty. During the Civil War she was living in Dublin at 51 Fitzwilliam Square where she sheltered wanted anti-Treaty IRA men, including Harry Boland, and worked as a courier for Oscar Traynor, O/C of the anti-Treaty IRA's Dublin Brigade during the Civil War.

Beatrice (Beanie) Brady, like her sisters, went to school at the St Louis Convent and then attended university at University College Dublin. She qualified as an accountant and in 1919 she began work as an auditor in Dáil Éireann. She was also a courier for Michael Collins during the War of Independence. She later became a nun in the Carmelite Order in Rathmines, Dublin.

Kathleen (Kay) Brady (*shown right with her mother*) was educated in Loreto College, St Stephen's Green, Dublin, and also Queen's University, Belfast, from where she graduated with an arts degree, Trinity College, Dublin and University College, Dublin. She was a secondary school teacher and, like her sister Frank, joined Cumann na mBan in 1916. She became very close friends with Ned Daly and Austin Stack. She was later elected to the executive of Cumann na mBan and during the War of Independence she lived at 46 Lower Leeson Street which was regularly used by the IRA as their headquarters. It was also from her home that the Belfast Boycott was organised. Kay opposed the Treaty. At the time of the attack on the Four Courts on 28 June 1922 she was in Belfast working on behalf of Cumann na mBan. She immediately returned to Dublin and served with the anti-Treaty IRA garrison in the Gresham Hotel on O'Connell Street. She was arrested after the surrender on 5 July but escaped and resumed her work for the Republicans, driving anti-Treaty IRA men such as Ernie O'Malley and Todd Andrews to various locations around the country. She was again arrested in late 1922 and was imprisoned in Kilmainham Gaol and the NDU, from where she escaped on 7 May 1923. In October 1923 Kay was sent, at the request of Éamon de Valera, to America and Canada to raise money for the Republican Prisoners' Dependants' Fund. Kay Brady died on 27 June 1957. She is buried in Glasnevin Cemetery alongside her sister Frank. (*Courtesy of Eithne Brady*)

On 2 April 1920 American women picketed the British Embassy in Washington in support of the cause of Irish freedom. They were prohibited by the police from marching to the embassy. (*Courtesy of Military Archives, IE-MA-BMH-CD-94/6/1*)

Undeterred the women returned the next day, Saturday 3 April. This time the police did not intervene. The women continued their protest and on 7 April they threw leaflets from an aeroplane flying over the British Embassy. (*Courtesy of the National Library of Ireland*)

Women picket outside the British Embassy in Washington in protest at the actions of the British government and crown forces in Ireland. (*Courtesy of the Library of Congress, LC-DIG-npcc-01352*)

Kathleen O'Brennan (*front*) was the sister of Áine Ceannt and Lily O'Brennan. She was working as a journalist in Washington and was a member of the 'American Women's Pickets' organisation. She took part in the many demonstrations organised by the women in protest at what was happening in Ireland. Kathleen was arrested in Washington for putting up posters all over the city denouncing the British government. (*Courtesy of the National Library of Ireland*)

In November 1920 the protests continued in New York and in one incident an Irish woman climbed a ladder to remove a Union Jack flag that was flying from the Capitol Theatre on Broadway. The woman succeeded in

removing the flag and then threw it to the waiting crowd who proceeded to destroy it. (*Courtesy of the Library of Congress, LC-DIG-npcc-01722*)

Female American support also came in more practical forms. This photograph shows the organising committee of the Irish White Cross, which enrolled more than 100 nurses in America who were willing to go to Ireland to help in the revolution. Most of these women were Irish-Americans. Seated on the floor (*left to right*): Margaret McHale, Jennie Ward, Margaret Dunn, Elizabeth Maguire and Josephine McHale. Sitting: Mary M. Hogan, Helen Fitzgerald, Bridget Reid, Mrs V. O. de Lisser, Mary Donogan, Eileen Fahy, Mary E. Buckley and Kathleen Hale. Standing: Beatrice Connolly, Kathleen McMahon, Maria Fitzgerald, Catherine Carberry, Anna M. Buckley, May F. Connolly, Anastasia Grattan, Margaret McCarthy and Josephine Reilly. (*Courtesy of the National Library of Ireland*)

Mary MacSwiney's brother Terence was arrested for sedition in 1920 and was imprisoned in Brixton Prison. He went on hunger strike, dying in October after seventy-four days. After Terence's death Mary and her sister-in-law Muriel went to America and both testified before the American Commission in Washington which was set up to investigate what was happening in Ireland (*pictured above*). On 21 December Muriel was given the Freedom of the City of New York. Many female relations of IRA men who had been executed or died in the conflict went to America to testify before the commission and the commission sent a delegation to Ireland to investigate the situation. They were accompanied by women like Charlotte Despard, who showed them the reality of the conflict throughout the country.

Mary returned to Ireland in early 1921 and was elected as a TD to Dáil Éireann. Muriel returned shortly after Mary and settled in Dublin. She opposed the Treaty and when the Civil War began she assisted the anti-Treaty IRA garrison in the Hammam Hotel. She was not arrested and in late 1922 returned to America as one of the numerous female anti-Treaty representatives engaged in a lecture tour to raise support for the movement. Muriel died in 1982 at the age of ninety. (*Courtesy of Library of Congress, LC-DIG-npcc-03131*)

By 1920 Cumann na mBan was well established in Co. Longford. Margaret (*above*), Maureen and Brighid McGuinness were members of the Longford Branch. They came from a staunch Republican family and were the nieces of Frank and Joseph McGuinness, who were both dedicated to the cause of Irish freedom. Joseph was a member of the 1st Battalion, Dublin Brigade, and had fought in the Easter Rising alongside two of his other nieces, Rose McGuinness and Brigid Lyons.

The McGuinness girls lived with their Uncle Frank in Main Street, Longford town. He owned two shops there, one selling boots and the other a drapers. The girls were influenced from a very young age by their uncles' political outlook and after the Easter Rising they joined Cumann na mBan. Their shop in Main Street was a hub of activity and one of the main intelligence centres for the Longford IRA Brigade. During the War of Independence the girls regularly put themselves in great danger transporting weapons and ammunition by train from Dublin to Longford. From their shop they gathered intelligence on the movements of the crown forces and would take photographs from the upper window of the premises of the soldiers, and later Auxiliaries (*pictured*), parading through the town. The family was known to the authorities and the girls would routinely be searched on trips to and from Dublin. During one such trip in 1921, Margaret was arrested and was imprisoned in Mountjoy. She was released after four months.

The McGuinness family supported the Treaty, as did most of the Longford IRA and Cumann na mBan. Margaret later married Richard Callanan, a veteran of the Longford IRA Brigade and later a member of the National Army. (*Courtesy of the McGuinness Collection*)

Top: Members of the McGuinness family campaign for their uncle Joe, Sinn Féin candidate for Longford in the 1918 general election. This photograph was taken in Main Street, Longford. Katie McGuinness (Joe's wife), sits in the car, centre back row. To her right is Brighid McGuinness and to her left Brigid Lyons Thornton (wearing glasses) and Maureen McGuinness, in front of Brigid Lyons Thornton.

Bottom right: Brighid McGuinness.

Bottom left (*left to right*): Maureen McGuinness, unidentified, Brighid and Margaret McGuinness. (*Courtesy of the McGuinness Collection*)

Lucy Fleming was born in 1885 in Mount Brown, Dublin, then moved with her family to the Ranch in nearby Ballyfermot. She worked in Inchicore Railway Works and was a member of the Central Branch of Cumann na mBan. Inchicore, the Ranch and Ballyfermot were right in the heart of the 4th Battalion, Dublin Brigade area and were well-known areas for having Republican sympathisers.

Lucy was to prove a vital asset during the War of Independence. She was the proud owner of an open-top Citroën car, a rarity in those days. Even more unusual was the fact that the car was owned by a woman. Because of this she was called on to transport supplies and weapons, and on one occasion was asked to go to Drogheda to collect guns which had been brought to Ireland in a German U-boat. She carried out the task alone and was successful in bringing the weapons back to the Ranch for the local IRA.

In 1924 Lucy went to Chicago where she got a teaching degree. She returned to Ireland in 1930 and took over the running of her mother's dairy shop in the Ranch. Lucy Fleming died in 1954. She was sixty-nine years old. (*Courtesy of Sé and Noel Fleming*)

Throughout the war money had to be raised for the IRA, mainly for weapons and ammunition. This work was mostly carried out by Cumann na mBan, who would stand outside local churches in their communities to collect money and carry out other activities such as selling flags. It was illegal to do this without a permit and many women, like the two women shown in the photograph, were arrested for doing so. (*Courtesy of James Langton*)

Margaret Collins was from Abbeyfeale in Co. Limerick and was vital to the West Limerick Brigade IRA during the War of Independence. She gathered information on the activities of the crown forces while also carrying dispatches between the local battalion leaders and the flying column. She was the sweetheart of James J. Collins, brigade adjutant of the West Limerick Brigade, and often carried messages from him to various people as he was wanted by the authorities. Margaret and James married after the Truce in 1921. This photograph shows Margaret in Áras an Uachtaráin with President Éamon de Valera, who was a close friend. (*Courtesy of Seán Collins*)

Sarah Ellen Bow was born in 1901 in Cloughjordan, Co. Tipperary. She joined Cumann na mBan after the Easter Rising. During the War of Independence she was a courier for the IRA, transporting weapons from brigade headquarters in Dublin to the various IRA units in Tipperary. She was never caught by the authorities, but her family home came under suspicion and in 1921 her house was burned down by the Black and Tans as part of their reprisal for an IRA ambush on a patrol of RIC and Tans at Modreeny, near Cloughjordan on 3 June, in which four RIC men were killed. Sarah Ellen Bow died in 1990, aged eighty-nine. (*Courtesy of Anne and Éire Garvey and Margaret Curtain*)

Madge Hales, from Ballinadee, Bandon, Co. Cork, came from a Republican family and all of her brothers – Seán, Tom, Robert, Liam and Dónal – were involved in the Republican movement, having joined the Volunteers at their inception. Tom Hales was O/C of the 3rd West Cork Brigade until his arrest in July 1920, while Seán was O/C of the Bandon Battalion. Madge was a courier for Michael Collins and took regular trips to Italy to her brother Dónal, who was a Republican envoy in Genoa. She went to secure arms and also to give Dónal information which he could use for propaganda purposes on behalf of the Republican movement.

However, the Hales family was to pay a high price for the cause of Irish freedom. In the Civil War the family was divided over the issue of the Treaty. Both Madge and Seán took the pro-Treaty side, while Tom, Robert, Liam and Dónal took the anti-Treaty side. Tom was involved in the ambush at Béal na mBláth in which Michael Collins was killed, while Seán was shot and killed in Dublin on 7 December 1922. Tom, Robert and Liam were all arrested during the Civil War. Fortunately, after the Civil War ended the family managed to reconcile their differences. Madge married Seamus Murphy and they had three children, one boy and two girls. (*Courtesy of Sean Hales*)

Lucy Agnes Smyth was born on 26 September 1882. She joined Cumann na mBan upon its inception and was a member of the Central (Árd Craobh) Branch where she became a section leader and later a 1st lieutenant. During the Rising she served in both the GPO and the Hibernian Bank, where she carried out first aid duties and delivered dispatches. On the morning of 24 April she mobilised other members of Cumann na mBan and that evening removed rifles from a house in Hardwick Street that was later raided. She stayed with the garrison in the GPO until Friday 29 April when she, with other members of Cumann na mBan, were ordered to remove the wounded to nearby Jervis Street Hospital. She evaded arrest and helped Volunteer Tom Byrne (Boer Tom) escape. Tom had fought in the GPO after he had led a contingent of Volunteers from Maynooth to take part in the fighting.

In the aftermath of the Rising Lucy helped in the reorganisation of the movement. She worked for the INAAVDF. On 28 April 1919 Lucy and Tom Byrne were married. Tom was now commandant of the 1st Battalion, Dublin Brigade, IRA. Due to the couple's nationalist activities their home was constantly raided by the authorities. In December 1919 Lucy became pregnant with her first child, but ten days after a raid by the crown forces in February 1920, in which Tom was arrested, Lucy lost her baby. Tom was later imprisoned in Wormwood Scrubs Prison, England. Upon regaining her health Lucy resumed her work for the Republican movement and in 1921 she began working in the Department of Labour. During this time her husband Tom remained in prison. She was later transferred to the Army Organisation Department and, also during the War of Independence, she served on the District Council of Cumann na mBan. Lucy did not take part in the Civil War. She and Tom went on to have four children. Lucy died in 1972. She was ninety years old. (*Courtesy of Sheila and Maeve O'Leary*)

Anna McNulty (née McCusker) was born in Scotland in 1890 and attended boarding school in London. Her family originally came from Dromore, Co. Tyrone and when she was eighteen years old she met and fell in love with John McNulty, a native of Dromore. They married in 1910 and bought a farm in Longhill, Dromore. Despite living in an area hostile to Republicans, Anna and John both contributed to the revolutionary movement. Anna herself often transported weapons and bombs from Omagh to Dromore. She would hide the bombs in the muff that she wore. Her home in Longhill was always available for IRA men who were on the run. Because of this she ran the risk of becoming known to the authorities and her house was raided a number of times by the Black and Tans. Despite this risk Anna and her husband continued to help in whatever way they could. She was captain of the Dromore Branch, Cumann na mBan and also president of the District Council, a position she held until July 1922.

Anna opposed the Treaty and remained an ardent Republican. In the 1930s she was a verifying officer for those who were applying for the Military Service Pension. Anna herself applied for both a pension and medal for her contribution to the War of Independence and, after much delay, she was successful in receiving both. (*Courtesy of Mrs Josephine Clarke*)

Kate McGovern and Seán Sheehan on their wedding day, June 1920, Dublin. Kate McGovern was from Glangevlin, Co. Cavan and worked as a nurse in Enniskillen, where she met Seán, who was a member of the IRA. During the War of Independence Kate used her job as a nurse to help the IRA, hiding weapons underneath hospital beds while also transporting weapons to Dublin. Seán and Kate had nine children and lived in Blackrock, Co. Dublin. They are both buried in Deansgrange Cemetery, Dublin. (*Courtesy of Kilmainham Gaol Archives, 2011.0275*)

Josephine (Josie) Stallard from Kilkenny was living in Dublin studying to be a doctor when the Easter Rising broke out. Her brothers were Volunteers and after the Rising she organised for wounded Volunteers to go to her family home in Kilkenny to be treated. While at home that summer she met Liam Clarke, a member of the Dublin Brigade who had fought in the GPO during the Rising and was wounded when a grenade he was carrying exploded in his face.

When Josie returned to Dublin, she joined both the Central Branch and University Branch of Cumann na mBan. She qualified as a doctor in May 1921. During the War of Independence she was a dispatch carrier to Liverpool for Cathal Brugha. Both she and Liam were arrested during June 1921 but, as no incriminating evidence was found on her, Josie was released. Liam was imprisoned in Arbour Hill Prison and Kilmainham Gaol. As a result of his earlier wound, Liam had to undergo medical treatment on his face and while out on parole receiving treatment, he and Josie were married in University church, Dublin (*their wedding day is shown here*) and honeymooned in Greystones. Her family did not support the marriage and did not speak to Josie for over a year. When his parole was up Liam returned to Kilmainham and was released under the general amnesty after the signing of the Treaty in December 1921.

Both Liam and Josie opposed the Treaty and were active in the Civil War. Liam fought in 'The Block' in O'Connell Street, while Josie set up a first aid station in Grand Canal Street. They went to Rathfarnham after the fighting in the city ended, where Josie set up a first aid post. She was joined by other members of Cumann na mBan, who brought the men much-needed weapons. The couple moved on to Blessington and with Kathleen Barry and seven other women they looked after the wounded. Josie was a few months pregnant at the time. Liam was again arrested and Josie returned to her family home in Kilkenny until his release. (*Courtesy of Fergus White*)

Crowds of women gather outside Mountjoy Prison on the morning of Thomas Traynor's execution. Traynor was arrested on 14 March at the 'Battle of Brunswick Street'. Tried by court martial, he was hanged in Mountjoy Prison on 25 April 1921. At 7.30 that morning members of Cumann na mBan from all over the city arrived at the prison and held a vigil for the condemned man. They had marched in formation through the city, four deep, and upon reaching the prison they recited the Rosary in Irish until 8 a.m. when the execution took place. After this they obtained Traynor's last message to the people and had copies printed, which they then posted up all over the city. (*Courtesy of Mercier Archive*)

Despite the fact that so many IRA men were on the run, they still found time to relax with their counterparts in Cumann na mBan at céilís and concerts, trying to live some sort of a normal life despite fighting a war, as can be seen in this photograph. Georgina Stella Archer (*middle row, behind man wearing hat*) was born in Dublin in 1900. She joined Cumann na mBan in 1917 and was a member of the Colmcille Branch. (*Courtesy of Kilmainham Gaol Archives, 19PO-1A33-1*)

Dan Breen met Brighid Malone when he stayed at her mother's house in Dublin in 1919. Brighid nursed Dan after he was wounded during the ambush at Ashtown in December 1919 and the two fell in love. Brighid's brother was Lieutenant Michael Malone, who was killed in action at the Battle of Mount Street Bridge during the Rising, and both Brighid and her sister Áine were members of Cumann na mBan. During the War of Independence she carried dispatches and weapons for the IRA and her home in Grantham Street was used as a safe house by the IRA. Brighid had to transport weapons from Dublin to Tipperary and was also actively engaged in ambushes carried out by the IRA. In the aftermath of 'Bloody Sunday' she was on hand to collect the guns from the Volunteers who had taken part in the morning's assassinations and had to hide the weapons. In February 1921 Brighid assisted in the escape of Frank Teeling, Ernie O'Malley and Simon Donnelly from Kilmainham Gaol. While carrying out these duties she also worked for the solicitor Michael Noyk, a Republican sympathiser.

Brighid and Dan were married on 21 June 1921 in Tipperary, and the couple are shown here on their wedding day, with the best man Seán Hogan and Brighid's sister Áine, who was bridesmaid. Dan Breen was one of the most wanted men in Ireland at the time, so the couple had to be very careful, but with the help of friends and comrades they were able to get married. The ceremony was held in the home of Michael Purcell near Clonmel after which the party moved to Jack Luby's of Milltown House. Tipperary was one of the most active areas in the country and had a large presence of military and police. Scouts from the 3rd Tipperary Brigade were posted around the whole area keeping watch for any military activity. The couple spent their honeymoon in Donohill, moving from house to house as it was too dangerous to stay in one place.

Brighid opposed the Treaty and during the Civil War she was attached to the headquarters staff of Seán Moylan, anti-Treaty IRA, in Clonmel. She carried dispatches for both Moylan and Liam Lynch, commander-in-chief of the anti-Treaty IRA. She returned to Dublin in 1923 where she continued to carry dispatches for the anti-Treaty IRA. She was never arrested. (*Courtesy of Mercier Archive*)

In July 1921 the British government called for a Truce with the Republicans. Talks took place between General Macready, representing the British government, and the Irish delegates in the Mansion House, Dublin. This photograph shows women reciting the Rosary outside the Mansion House, during the talks. Over a number of days discussions took place and crowds would gather outside daily waiting for news. Agreement was reached and the Truce came into effect at 12 noon on 11 July 1921, ending the War of Independence. (*Courtesy of Military Archives, IE-MA-BMH-CD-250-5-5*)

During the Truce period, many in both the IRA and the crown forces believed that the Truce would not last long and that hostilities could resume at any time. Although the terms of the Truce stated that recruitment and training for the IRA was to stop, the IRA ignored this and used this time as a chance to train, drill and reorganise the brigades throughout the country. Training camps were set up and were attended by both the IRA and Cumann na mBan, as shown in these photographs taken at a training camp in Ballinard, Co. Tipperary. (*Image above courtesy of Martin O'Dwyer; image opposite courtesy of Mercier Archive*)

Linda Kearns (*right*) was born in Sligo in 1889. She trained to be a nurse in the Royal City of Dublin Hospital, Baggot Street, and planned to go to Europe during the war to help. However, having met Thomas MacDonagh she decided instead to stay and help in Ireland and, although not a member of Cumann na mBan, during the Rising she was asked to set up a hospital in North Great Georges Street to treat wounded Volunteers. She avoided arrest and during the Spanish Flu epidemic she helped treat the sick while also carrying messages and ammunition between Sligo and Mayo at the request of Michael Collins. She ran a nursing home with her sister in Gardiner Place, Dublin, which was also used as a safe house by Volunteers on the run. She later returned to Sligo and carried on her work for the IRA.

During the War of Independence, Linda Kearns was one of the few people to own a car, which made her invaluable to the IRA in moving weapons throughout Sligo. An order was brought in by the British that anyone found carrying weapons could be executed. She was arrested in November 1920 while escorting three IRA men and their weapons from a proposed ambush, and to save the lives of her comrades she claimed the weapons were hers. All of them were taken into custody and Kearns was beaten during her interrogation. She was held in various jails including Sligo, Derry, Belfast and Armagh, before being found guilty at her trial and sentenced to ten years in prison. She was sent to Liverpool to serve out her sentence. While there she began a hunger strike in protest at being held in England and was successful in getting sent back to Mountjoy Prison in Dublin. She was not long there when she began to plan her escape. In October 1921, along with Eithne Coyle (*centre*), Eileen Keogh and Mae Burke (*left*), she escaped from Mountjoy and got safely away to an IRA training camp in Duckett's Grove, Co. Carlow. This photograph shows Linda, Mae and Eithne during their stay in Duckett's Grove. (*Courtesy of Delia McDevitt*)

Kathleen McKenna (*centre*) was a typist and worked in the Dáil Éireann propaganda department from November 1919 until the Truce in July 1921. She worked on the daily Republican newssheet *The Irish Bulletin*, which was first published in November 1919 to counteract British reports of the war. Throughout the war the *Bulletin* was issued every day. The work was completed by a staff of six, initially under the direction of Desmond Fitzgerald, director of propaganda. Once their work came to the attention of the authorities they constantly had to move office to avoid arrest. McKenna's work included not only typing the contents of the paper but also collecting material from locations around the city. She was living in Belvedere Road with her father and despite working all day in the office, in order to ensure that an issue was not missed she would often have to type up the 'Weekly Summary of Aggressions' for the *Bulletin* in the dead of night in her home. She also had a duplicating machine in her house, which was later raided but fortunately she was not there.

In their temporary office in Molesworth Street the staff often had to work in the cold. She and Anna Fitzsimmons often had to put blotting paper around their stockings to dry them out and keep warm. When the British Army moved to occupy the crown solicitor's office, which was beneath the *Bulletin* office, as their headquarters, Kathleen and the other women had to get wanted IRA men out of the office as a cordon was put up around the area. They got the men and also valuable documents away successfully, as well as removing their equipment in full view of the soldiers. Prior to the Truce, despite having offices on Rathgar Road, Kathleen continued to publish the *Bulletin* from her home, ensuring that it was issued every day.

Kathleen was chosen as one of the secretaries to the Irish delegation during the Treaty negotiations and is seen here getting off the boat at Holyhead to attend the talks along with (*left to right*) Alice Lyons, Ellie Lyons and Robert Barton. (*Courtesy of Mercier Archive*)

The Treaty negotiations between the British government and the Irish delegation began on 11 October 1921. There was a great deal of thought put into choosing who should accompany the delegation as their secretaries. All of the women chosen to go had proven themselves more than capable of carrying out their work, having worked in similar positions in more trying circumstances during the War of Independence.

Some members of the delegation are shown here in Hans Place, London, on their return from their first day of talks. Front row (*left to right*): Lily O'Brennan (Childers' typist, sister of Áine Ceannt), Ellie Lyons, May Kavanagh (Mrs Éamon Duggan), Bridget Slattery (Mrs Fionán Lynch), Kathleen McKenna, Alice Lyons, Fionán Lynch (secretary). Second row: Joe McGrath, Captain David Robinson. Third row: Mick Knightly (official reporter), John Chartres (secretary), George Gavan Duffy, Robert Barton, Ned Duggan, Arthur Griffith, Erskine Childers. (*Courtesy of Mercier Archive*)

Left to right: Alice Lyons, Kathleen McKenna and Ellie Lyons. The women carry out their secretarial duties in Hans Place during the negotiations. (*Courtesy of Mercier Archive*)

The secretaries take a break from their work. After much discussion and under the threat of 'terrible and immediate war' from the British, the Irish delegates signed the Anglo-Irish Treaty in the early hours of 6 December 1921. (*Courtesy of Mercier Archive*)

Charlotte Despard (*second from right*) and Maud Gonne (*fourth from right*) liaise with British soldiers outside Mountjoy Prison in 1921.

Charlotte Despard (née French) was born in Kent to Captain John Tracey William French, a retired British naval officer, and Margaret Eccles. In 1870 she married Maximilian Despard, a wealthy Anglo-Irish businessman. Maximilian died in 1890, after which Charlotte immersed herself in philanthropic ventures. She also became involved in politics, joining the Social Democratic Federation and the Independent Labour Party and becoming involved with the suffragette movement. In 1906 she joined the Women's Social and Political Union and, when it split in 1907, the Women's Freedom League (WFL). On the outbreak of the First World War she joined the socialist pacifist movement.

In 1918 she resigned as president of the WFL in order to devote her energies to other causes, including the Irish Self-Determination League, an organisation set up to gain support from the Irish population living in Britain for Irish independence. In 1918 Charlotte's brother, Sir John French, became lord lieutenant of Ireland. While he was determined to crush Republican resistance to British rule, Charlotte fully supported the Republicans. During the War of Independence, she received many letters to intervene with her brother on behalf of Irishmen who were imprisoned. One such letter from Maud Gonne resulted in her travelling to Ireland in January 1921 to see for herself what was happening. There she met Gonne and the two became close friends. Charlotte moved to Ireland permanently in the summer of 1921. She travelled all over the country visiting towns and villages that had come under attack from the crown forces as reprisals for ambushes carried out by the IRA against the British forces. As Charlotte highlighted through these visits, it was the ordinary civilians, and particularly the women of these communities, who bore the brunt of these attacks. With Maud Gonne, Charlotte would also accompany women to the prison their husband, son or brother was being held in, giving support and whatever help she could offer.

In August 1922, after the outbreak of the Civil War, Charlotte and Gonne set up the Women's Prisoners' Defence League, of which Charlotte was president. Maud Gonne was arrested during the Civil War and, despite being seventy-nine years old, Charlotte kept a vigil outside Kilmainham Gaol where Gonne was being held. (*Courtesy of South County Dublin Library*)

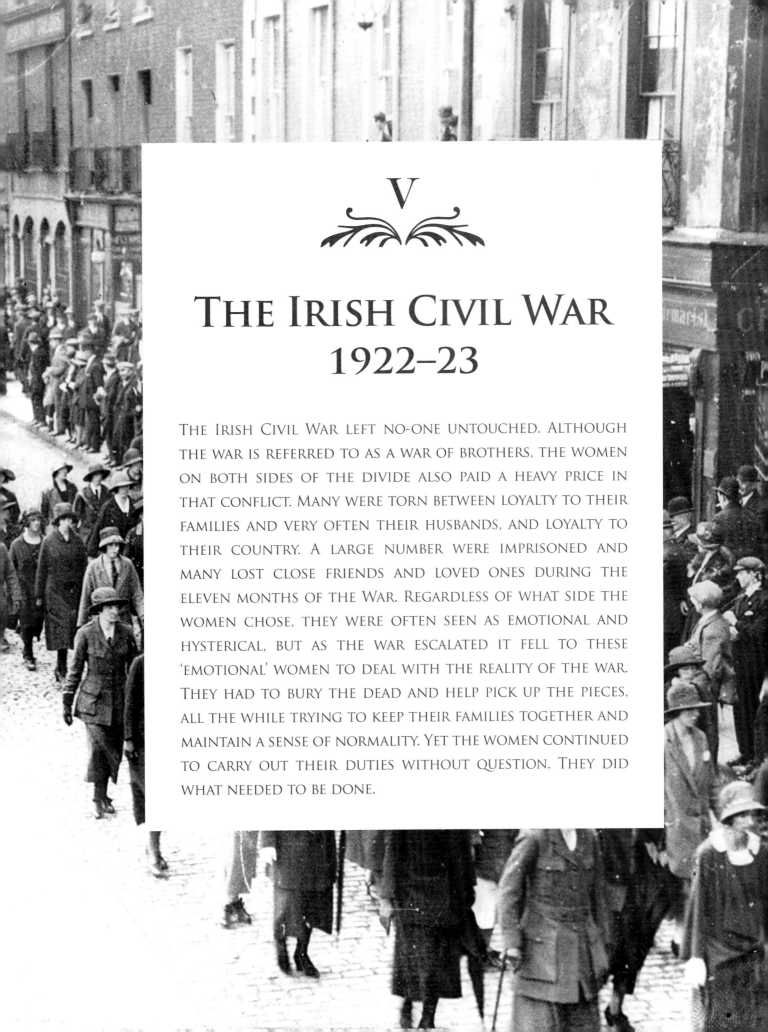

V

THE IRISH CIVIL WAR
1922–23

THE IRISH CIVIL WAR LEFT NO-ONE UNTOUCHED. ALTHOUGH
THE WAR IS REFERRED TO AS A WAR OF BROTHERS, THE WOMEN
ON BOTH SIDES OF THE DIVIDE ALSO PAID A HEAVY PRICE IN
THAT CONFLICT. MANY WERE TORN BETWEEN LOYALTY TO THEIR
FAMILIES AND VERY OFTEN THEIR HUSBANDS, AND LOYALTY TO
THEIR COUNTRY. A LARGE NUMBER WERE IMPRISONED AND
MANY LOST CLOSE FRIENDS AND LOVED ONES DURING THE
ELEVEN MONTHS OF THE WAR. REGARDLESS OF WHAT SIDE THE
WOMEN CHOSE, THEY WERE OFTEN SEEN AS EMOTIONAL AND
HYSTERICAL, BUT AS THE WAR ESCALATED IT FELL TO THESE
'EMOTIONAL' WOMEN TO DEAL WITH THE REALITY OF THE WAR.
THEY HAD TO BURY THE DEAD AND HELP PICK UP THE PIECES,
ALL THE WHILE TRYING TO KEEP THEIR FAMILIES TOGETHER AND
MAINTAIN A SENSE OF NORMALITY. YET THE WOMEN CONTINUED
TO CARRY OUT THEIR DUTIES WITHOUT QUESTION. THEY DID
WHAT NEEDED TO BE DONE.

Left to right: Kathleen Clarke, Countess Markievicz, Kate O'Callaghan and Mrs Pearse attending the Treaty debates in Dublin. All four women were TDs, having been elected to the second Dáil. During the Treaty debates between December 1921 and January 1922, the women each addressed the Dáil and spoke of why the Treaty should be rejected. For many of the women who had lost loved ones in the Easter Rising and War of Independence, acceptance of the Treaty was not an option. They had suffered and endured terrible hardship and would accept that loss for a Republic, but not for a Free State. Kathleen Clarke's husband Tom and her brother Ned were both executed after the Easter Rising. Kate O'Callaghan, a member of Cumann na mBan in Limerick, saw her husband Michael, an officer of the Limerick IRA and lord mayor of Limerick, murdered by the crown forces in March 1921. (*Courtesy of the Pearse Museum, 2004.0196*)

Mary MacSwiney opposed the Treaty and during the Treaty debates she addressed the Dáil, speaking at length on why it should not be accepted. Her first arrest came in November 1922 when she was staying in Nancy O'Rahilly's house. MacSwiney was taken to Mountjoy Prison and began a hunger strike soon after. Her sister-in-law Muriel is shown here protesting her incarceration. Mary was released but was rearrested in April 1923 while going to the funeral of Liam Lynch – the authorities were afraid she would use this as a platform to attack the Free State government. Imprisoned in Kilmainham Gaol, she once again went on hunger strike and was released in May 1923. She was elected to the Dáil in the elections of 1923 but refused to take her seat and continued in her work with Cumann na mBan. In 1924 MacSwiney was one of a number of women who went to America on a fund-raising tour for the Republican movement. Although she had supported de Valera in his stance on the Treaty, she did not support him when he left Sinn Féin to set up Fianna Fáil. Mary MacSwiney remained a committed Republican for the rest of her life. She died in 1942, aged seventy. (*Courtesy of Library of Congress, LC-DIG-npcc-07316*)

Left to right: unidentified, Sorcha Duggan (president of Cork District Council, Cumann na mBan), Kate Breen (*front*) (member of Cumann na mBan executive, Dublin), Lil Conlon (Shandon Branch, Cumann na mBan), May Conlon (Shandon Branch, Cumann na mBan and honorary secretary of Cork District Council), unidentified. The Treaty was ratified by Dáil Éireann by a narrow majority, 64 to 57 votes, on 7 January 1922. Cumann na mBan was the first organisation to hold a convention to put the issue to its members. The convention was held on 5 February in the Mansion House and, after much debate, the organisation voted not to accept the Treaty by 419 votes to 63. The women, just like the IRA and Sinn Féin, were unable to reconcile their differences and the inevitable split went right to the top of the organisation. Although the majority of the branches were anti-Treaty, Cork was the exception, with many of the branches there accepting the Treaty. Both sides continued to call themselves Cumann na mBan, which often led to heated exchanges especially between Mary MacSwiney, member of the executive, and May Conlon, honorary secretary, both of Cork. Conlon was informed by Cumann na mBan headquarters in Dublin that she and her supporters were no longer members of Cumann na mBan and should cease to use the name. She ignored the order. (*Courtesy of Cork Public Museum*)

On 12 March 1922 the Cork pro-Treaty Cumann na mBan organised a Tableau and concert at the Cork Opera House in honour of Michael Collins. On Collins' arrival at Glanmire railway station, Cork city, he was greeted on a platform decorated with flags and bunting by Cumann na mBan who lined up in formation while May Conlon read an address to Collins in Irish for the occasion. (*Courtesy of Cork Public Museum*)

Lily O'Brennan, sister of Áine Ceannt, was born in Dublin in 1878. She was a writer and playwright and joined Cumann na mBan upon its inception as a member of the Inghinidhe Branch. During the Rising she served with the Marrowbone Lane garrison. She was arrested and held in Kilmainham Gaol and was released on 8 May, the day her brother-in-law, Éamonn Ceannt, was executed in the gaol. She continued to be involved in the Republican movement and was a clerk for the Irish National Aid Association, which later amalgamated with the Irish Volunteer Dependants' Fund. She also worked at this time locating the graves of Volunteers killed during the Rising and marking them. A member of Sinn Féin, she was co-opted onto its executive committee as well as being a member of the executive of Cumann na mBan.

During the War of Independence Lily was a district judge in the Republican Courts, while also working for the Dáil's Department of Labour. With Eilís Ní Riain, she was responsible for ensuring the safety of wounded Volunteers and upon receiving word of an impending raid it was their job to get the men away to another hospital, usually late at night. She oversaw the Belfast Boycott in Dublin and at the time of the Treaty negotiations she was private secretary to Arthur Griffith. She opposed the Treaty and became secretary to Erskine Childers.

During the Civil War Lily carried dispatches between the Sinn Féin offices in 23 Suffolk Street and the Four Courts. She also helped set up a hospital in Suffolk Street, sheltered wanted anti-Treaty IRA men and also helped with anti-Treaty propaganda. Lily was asked by Childers to meet him in Cork where he was carrying out his propaganda work. She was arrested in October 1922 and was imprisoned in Mountjoy Prison and the NDU. She was released in July 1923 and resumed her work with her anti-Treaty colleagues, helping campaign for the general election that year. Throughout all of this activity she also carried out work for the White Cross.

In later life Lily took to writing plays and short stories for adults and children in both English and Irish, and was a founding member of the Catholic Writers' Guild. She died in 1948, aged seventy. (*Courtesy of the National Library of Ireland*)

Brigid Lyons was born in 1898. Originally from Sligo, she went to live with her uncle, Joe McGuinness, in Co. Longford when she was eight years old. He was involved in the nationalist movement and, following her uncle's political ideals, Brigid joined Cumann na mBan soon after its inception. She came to Dublin during Easter Week and took part in the Rising, serving alongside her cousin, Rose McGuinness, in the Four Courts, where she helped feed the garrison. She was arrested after the surrender and taken to Richmond Barracks and Kilmainham Gaol, but was released on 9 May. She was eighteen years old. She quickly resumed her work with Cumann na mBan while studying medicine. She helped campaign for Sinn Féin in the 1918 general election and also raised money for the Prisoners' Dependants' Fund.

During the War of Independence Brigid transported weapons for the IRA in Galway and was later transferred to the Longford Brigade IRA, where she helped buy weapons and ammunition for the brigade. She qualified as a doctor in 1922. She supported the Treaty and helped set up the Irish Army Medical Service in 1922. During the Civil War she was the medical officer in charge of Kilmainham Gaol, looking after the anti-Treaty female prisoners who were held there, many of whom were her former friends.

In 1926 she married Edward Thornton. Continuing with her career in medicine, she became state medical officer in the Department of Maternity and Child Welfare for Co. Dublin, later helping to introduce the BCG vaccination, and was part of the scheme to vaccinate children in order to combat the spread of tuberculosis. Brigid Lyons Thornton died in 1987. She was eighty-nine years old. (*Courtesy of the McGuinness Collection*)

In 1919 Min Ryan married Richard Mulcahy (*pictured together*), a noted Republican, but they had little time to enjoy their life as newlyweds as Richard was a wanted man and had to spend most of his time away from home. They had two children between 1919 and 1921 and, when possible, Richard would visit. Min went to Belfast to live with her sister Agnes, who was married to another IRA man, Denis McCullough. Min backed her husband in his support of the Treaty, as did her sister Agnes and her husband, despite the fact that their other siblings were against the Treaty.

The Civil War was to have a huge effect on the Ryan family. Min's sister Nell and brother Jim were both arrested and Nell went on hunger strike. Despite many pleas for Nell's release being made to her brother-in-law, Mulcahy refused to intervene as he could not be seen to give preferential treatment.

Unlike many families who were divided in their opinion of the Treaty and, as a result of the Civil War, could not reconcile in later life, the Ryans managed to heal the divide. This was mainly due to the fact that they had young families and believed that for the sake of their children they should put the past behind them, thus giving their children the chance to grow up knowing all their aunts and uncles. (*Courtesy of Elisabet Berney*)

Seán T. O'Kelly had known the Ryan family from the early days of the Volunteer movement. He and Kit Ryan were very close and married in 1918. Like her younger sister Min, Kit spent the early days of her married life separated from her husband. He was to spend most of the next four years in France as a Republican envoy, trying to get Ireland represented at the Paris Peace Conference after the First World War had ended. Kit remained in Dublin, teaching in UCD. Although she initially supported the Treaty, when her husband returned to Ireland in March 1922, she adopted his view by opposing it.

Kit Ryan died in 1934 of rheumatic heart disease, at the age of fifty-six. Two years later O'Kelly married another of the Ryan sisters – Phyllis, the youngest (*pictured*). She had grown up knowing Seán and all the other key figures in the revolutionary movement through her older sisters. She got her degree in chemistry in 1917 and set up a laboratory in Dawson Street, Dublin, where she worked as an analyst, and she ran this successfully for many years, employing many female graduates. As O'Kelly's wife she became first lady when he became the president of Ireland, serving two terms from 1945 to 1959. Phyllis Ryan died in 1983, aged eighty-eight. (*Courtesy of Military Archives, PC-59-3-6*)

The wedding of Pádraig O'Connor and Nellie O'Brien, 27 February 1922. Pádraig was a veteran of the War of Independence and a member of 'F' Company, 4th Battalion, Dublin Brigade, and the brigade's active service unit. Nellie was a member of Cumann na mBan and lived quite close to Pádraig, and was a friend of his sister Mary Jo. They met while she was helping to look after IRA men who were imprisoned. It would be quite a while before Pádraig and Nellie would get the chance to enjoy married life together, as Pádraig was to see action not just in Dublin at the beginning of the Civil War in June, but also in Tipperary and Cork as the war progressed. They had four children, one boy and three girls. Front row (*left to right*): Pádraig, Nellie, unidentified, Seán O'Connor. Middle row: General Paddy Daly, unidentified, General J. J. 'Ginger' O'Connell, Colonel Joe Leonard, Jim Harpur. (*Courtesy of Diarmuid O'Connor*)

As a result of the split in Cumann na mBan the pro-Treaty supporters formed a new organisation, Cumann na Saoirse (Freedom Group). In Cork they became known as Cumann na nGaedheal and just as they had assisted the IRA during the War of Independence, these women assisted the pro-Treaty forces in organising supplies of food, cigarettes and basic necessities for the soldiers. As the war progressed they regularly put on concerts and other entertainment in the hospitals for wounded soldiers. (*Courtesy of Cork Public Museum*)

Crowds gather at College Green to hear Michael Collins speak at a pro-Treaty rally, March 1922. During this rally Brighid O'Mullane and eleven members of the anti-Treaty Cumann na mBan succeeded in storming the platform and removing the Tricolour. They got away and evaded arrest. (*Courtesy of Mercier Archive*)

Sarah Mellows (née Jordan) was born in Monalug, Co. Wexford, in 1865 and was the mother of Liam, Barney and Frederick Mellows. Although she came from a staunch Republican family she married a British soldier, William Mellows, in 1885. Due to his career they moved all over Britain, returning to Ireland in 1895 and settling in Dublin, by which time they had one daughter and three boys who all later joined Na Fianna Éireann. Tragedy was never far away for Sarah and her family – she had already lost two children in infancy and her daughter Jane died of tuberculosis in 1914. She and her husband had very different political views, but it never affected their marriage.

Sarah was a founding member of Cumann na mBan and was closely associated with Na Fianna through Liam and Barney. She managed to see Liam before he set off for Galway for the Rising, but did not see him again for five years. After the Rising he went on the run, eventually escaping to America, while Barney was arrested and deported to England. Sarah's house near Kilmainham was a regular meeting place for Cumann na mBan as well as a safe house for Volunteers. In the aftermath of the Rising she delivered dispatches and weapons for the Volunteers, but was never suspected by the authorities. She was also involved in the INAAVDF as an organiser and fund-raiser, and during the War of Independence she often led demonstrations and protests outside the prisons, an activity that brought her to the attention of the police. Her husband, William, died in 1920.

Liam returned to Ireland in 1921 and when the Treaty was signed in December both he and Barney opposed it. Liam was a member of the anti-Treaty IRA executive and fought in the Four Courts at the outbreak of the Civil War in June 1922. Arrested after the surrender of the Courts, he was taken to Mountjoy with the other anti-Treaty IRA men who had fought in the Courts. On the evening of 7 December Sarah's house was raided by pro-Treaty forces looking for Barney, who was arrested that night and taken to Wellington Barracks. While on the way to see Barney the next morning she heard of Liam's execution in Mountjoy Prison. Barney was transferred to Hare Park internment camp and released in 1924.

After the Civil War Sarah went to America with Eamon Martin on a fund-raising tour. Her last surviving son, Barney, died in 1942, aged forty-six. Sarah died in December 1952, aged eighty-seven. She is just one example of the women of Ireland who made terrible sacrifices during that time, outliving all of her children and enduring the pain of seeing them imprisoned and executed for their country. She is buried in Glasnevin Cemetery. (*Courtesy of Kilmainham Gaol Archives, 20PC-1D31-26d*)

Máire Comerford (*centre*) was born in Rathdrum, Co. Wicklow, in 1893. She joined the Central Branch of Cumann na mBan as well as Sinn Féin in 1918, having become radicalised in the aftermath of the Easter Rising. She was soon appointed as an organiser for Cumann na mBan and was sent to Wexford to organise branches there. In 1920 she became O/C of the North Wexford Brigade, a post she held until 1923. Comerford was appointed to the General Council of the White Cross and organised for them all over the country distributing funds, while also acting as a courier for Michael Collins and an organiser for Cumann na mBan. She was appointed to the District Council and later to the executive of Cumann na mBan. She opposed the Treaty and before the Civil War began she was director of propaganda. She was in the Four Courts at the outbreak of fighting in June 1922 and carried dispatches between the Four Courts garrison and Oscar Traynor's command in 'The Block' in O'Connell Street. She avoided arrest and went south to Munster, but was eventually arrested and imprisoned in Mountjoy Prison, Kilmainham Gaol and the NDU. She was one of the women who managed to escape from the Union. She was re-arrested, went on hunger strike and after twenty-seven days was released. She campaigned in the general election of 1923 and was again arrested in Cork. Comerford was later smuggled to America, where she spent nine months fund-raising for the Republican cause. She was on the executive of Sinn Féin and did not support de Valera when he left the party in 1926. She returned to Wexford and ran a poultry farm. Over the next fifty years she was in and out of prison for various protests, and was a committed Republican right until the day she died. The last time she was arrested was in 1974, when she was eighty-one years old. Máire Comerford died in 1982, aged eighty-nine. (© *RTÉ Stills Library*)

Mrs Margaret Pearse speaking at Wolfe Tone's grave, Bodenstown, April 1922. Mrs Pearse and her daughter Margaret continued Patrick's work in keeping his school St Enda's (Scoil Éanna) running. Although she was not actively involved in the War of Independence and the Civil War that followed, Mrs Pearse gave great support to the Republican movement. St Enda's was always open to men who were on the run and many men who were released from prison would be sent there to recuperate. The grounds of the school were also often made available to the Volunteers for drill practice and training. Mrs Pearse opposed the Treaty and spoke in the debates that took place in Dáil Éireann on the subject. She continued to speak out against it and in the months leading up to the Civil War she would regularly speak at anti-Treaty rallies.

In 1924 Mrs Pearse was one of the many Republican women who went on a fund-raising trip to America on behalf of the Republicans. (*Courtesy of Mercier Archive*)

Members of the Cumann na mBan cyclist corps, Bodenstown, April 1922. Far right (*top*) is Máire Deegan. She was born in Wexford in 1891. She moved to Dublin where she worked as a shop assistant. Máire joined Cumann na mBan upon its inception and was a member of the Central Branch of which she later became 2nd lieutenant. On Easter Monday Máire cycled from Brideswell, Co. Wexford, to Dublin with a dispatch which she had hidden in her hair. She was to deliver the dispatch to Volunteer Headquarters in the GPO, which she did and stayed with the garrison carrying out first aid duties. She remained there until Friday, when the women were ordered to leave, and she evaded capture. During the 1918 general election Máire helped campaign for the Sinn Féin candidates. Soon afterwards, she and Máire O'Neill, another Cumann na mBan member, went into business together and opened a grocery shop in 95 Upper Dorset Street, Dublin. It was called Deegan and O'Neill and was used by the IRA as a message and dispatch centre. Despite being located in a well-known Republican area, the shop was never raided by the military. A keen cyclist, during the War of Independence Máire was an invaluable messenger for the IRA. She cycled all over the country bringing dispatches and provisions to the local IRA companies. In October 1920 Máire was elected onto the executive of Cumann na mBan.

Máire opposed the Treaty and upon the outbreak of the Civil War served initially with the anti-Treaty IRA in Barry's Hotel and later the Hammam Hotel, where she helped look after the men. She evaded arrest after the fighting in Dublin ended on 5 July and rather than stay in Dublin she accompanied the anti-Treaty forces making their way south in the hope of joining the main body of the anti-Treaty IRA. Returning to Dublin in November 1922, Máire was arrested and held in Mountjoy Prison. In February 1923 she was one of twelve women who went on hunger strike in Mountjoy to protest that their right to receive letters and parcels had been stopped by the governor of the prison, Paudeen O'Keeffe. The strike was called off after seven days and their privileges were reinstated.

On 3 May Máire was transferred to the NDU with the other fifty women from Mountjoy. She was elected to the Temporary Prisoners' Council in the NDU as censor. The Council was set up to organise liaisons with the authorities regarding the women's treatment in prison. Máire was not there for long. On 7 May, with Máire Comerford and Effie Taafe, Máire succeeded in escaping. She was re-arrested some time later.

When the Civil War ended Máire continued as a member of Cumann na mBan and was to remain an ardent Republican. In 1933 with Sighle Humphreys, Elgin Barry and Hannah Sheehy Skeffington, she succeeded in entering a building in Kildare Street which had the Union Jack flying from a window. They managed to seize the flag and set it alight. They were not arrested.

Máire lived on St Stephen's Green and worked in the civil service and also for a time with the Irish Sweepstakes. She died in May 1939. She was forty-eight years old. (*Courtesy of Military Archives, BMH CD 266-07-01*)

Annie Dempsey was from Rialto Buildings, Rialto, Dublin and was a volunteer nurse at the Sisters of Charity Hospice in Harold's Cross, Dublin. Michael Sweeney was a member of the 4th Battalion, Dublin Brigade IRA, and owned a garage in Harold's Cross. The two became acquainted during the War of Independence and fell in love. Through her relationship with Michael, Annie became very good friends with many IRA men, including Noel Lemass, Tom Cullen and Liam Tobin.

Michael opposed the Treaty and was arrested by pro-Treaty forces before the Civil War began. He was one of the first casualties of the Civil War – when he was being transferred from Mountjoy Prison he was mortally wounded in transit. Some reports claim he was trying to escape from custody.

Although Annie was not a member of Cumann na mBan, she was arrested in 1923, possibly due to her friendship with a number of those on the anti-Treaty side, and was imprisoned in Kilmainham Gaol. Annie was a typical example of just how tragic the Civil War was for Irish women. Not only did she lose her sweetheart in the conflict, but she lost many close friends, men from both sides of the divide. Annie later married Arthur Hughes, who worked for the Great Southern and Western Railways and had no connection with the revolutionary movement. They had three children, two girls and a boy, Bob, to whom she told the many stories of that period in her life. Annie Dempsey died in 1975. She was seventy-six years old. (*Courtesy of Bob Hughes*)

Ita O'Gorman, pictured here in her Cumann na mBan uniform, was born in 1902. She was member of Cumann na mBan and during the War of Independence befriended an officer in the Auxiliaries in order to gather intelligence for the IRA. Many women of Cumann na mBan carried out such work in this way and put themselves at great risk as they could be the target of attack from their own people who could assume they were consorting with the enemy. Ita was so effective in her work that one officer became so smitten with her that he asked her to visit his home in England. Ita opposed the Treaty and during the Civil War tended to wounded Republicans at Cullenswood House, Ranelagh, Dublin, the former home of Patrick Pearse. The group photograph shows her (*far right*) with other members of Cumann na mBan and wounded Republicans at Cullenswood House in July 1922. (*Courtesy of Kilmainham Gaol Archives, 19PC-1B52-17*)

Cumann na mBan march in the funeral cortège of Cathal Brugha (*opposite*) and form the guard of honour at his lying-in-state (*below*), 10 July 1922. Those who were asked to form the guard of honour were not told the names of the other women who were present. During this time a death mask of Brugha was made and it fell to the women to wash the remnants of plaster from his face. Hannah Dingley (*centre*) was a member of the Colmcille Branch of Cumann na mBan. She joined the organisation in 1918 and remained a member until the Civil War ended. She died in 1989, aged ninety.

Similar scenes were to be repeated all over the country during the Civil War. As the war escalated it was impossible for anti-Treaty IRA men to attend the funerals of their comrades. This task fell to Cumann na mBan, who came out in force to be the guard of honour at many funerals.

When the Civil War ended, thousands of anti-Treaty IRA men were imprisoned. During the war the Provisional Government officially executed seventy-seven Republicans and their bodies were not returned to their families until October 1924. As so many Republicans were still in prison, the responsibility for organising these funerals also fell to Cumann na mBan. They arranged the removal of the remains from the various prisons and barracks, and in most cases draped the coffins in Tricolours and accompanied the remains to the churches, again forming a guard of honour. (*Courtesy of Kilmainham Gaol Archives, 20PO-1A34-14* and *20PO-1A34-01*)

Mary Collins-Powell, sister of Michael Collins, visiting Béal na mBláth, Cork, the site of the fatal ambush where her brother was killed. Mary was a member of Cumann na mBan in Cork and in the aftermath of the Rising her home in Clonakilty came to the attention of the authorities. During the years of the War of Independence her home was regularly used by members of the IRA in West Cork who would leave messages for her younger brother. (*Courtesy of Military Archives, A. E. Lawlor Collection, PC 59*)

Nurses form a guard of honour at the removal of the remains of Michael Collins from St Vincent's Hospital, St Stephen's Green, Dublin, August 1922. (*Courtesy of the National Library Ireland, IND_H_0276 17079*).

Women on top of a carriage waving to prisoners in Mountjoy Prison. During the Civil War scenes like this were repeated all over the country. Daily the mothers, wives, sweethearts and sisters of imprisoned IRA men went to the prisons to get news of how their loved ones were. At Kilmainham Gaol the women would stand at the Camac Bridge while the prisoners would go to the top floor of the East Wing of the prison which overlooked the bridge, and they would communicate with each other, much like in the photograph here. As the Civil War escalated the Republican prisoners were forbidden from continuing this practice and often, after a warning to stop, shots were fired at the windows to prevent this – a number of Republicans were killed and wounded in this manner. (*Courtesy of Kilmainham Gaol Archives, 20PC-1A58-08*)

This photograph shows the wedding of Peadar Breslin and Annie Callender in Dublin *c.* 1920. Front row (*left to right*): Margaret and Tom Breslin; middle row: Mary Breslin, Annie Callender and Ignatius Callender; back row: Jamesie Breslin, Anne Callender, Peadar Breslin, Frank Callender, Annie Breslin.

Peadar was a member of 'G' Company, 1st Battalion, Dublin Brigade. He had fought in the North King Street area during the Easter Rising with his future brother-in-law, Ignatius Callender. He opposed the Treaty and fought with the Four Courts garrison at the outbreak of the Civil War. He was arrested after the surrender on 30 June and imprisoned in Mountjoy Prison. At this time he and Annie had a one-year-old son, Rory, and Annie was pregnant with their second child. On 11 October, while getting ready to bring Rory to Mountjoy to see his father, Annie received the news that Peadar had been shot and killed. There had been an attempted escape and in the ensuing commotion Peadar was hit by a ricochet bullet. Not long after her husband's death Annie gave birth to another son, whom she named Peadar. (*Courtesy of Peter McMahon and the Breslin family*)

This photograph of the wedding of Kevin O'Higgins and Brigid Mary Cole (*centre*) is a particularly poignant example of the tragedy unleashed by the Irish Civil War. O'Higgins met Brigid, an English teacher at St Mary's College, Knockbeg, through his work for Sinn Féin during the War of Independence and they were married in the Carmelite Church, Whitefriar Street, Dublin, on 27 October 1921. O'Higgins' best man was his best friend Rory O'Connor (*right*), but due to their opposing views on the Treaty they would become enemies less than two months after this photograph was taken. The other man in the photo, Éamon de Valera (*left*), would also take the anti-Treaty side. O'Connor, a member of the anti-Treaty IRA executive who took over the Four Courts in April 1922, was arrested and imprisoned after the surrender. Kevin O'Higgins confirmed the order for his execution, along with Joe McKelvey, Richard Barrett and Liam Mellows, in Mountjoy Prison on 8 December 1922 in response to the assassination of General Seán Hales of the National Army on 7 December. O'Higgins was himself assassinated in retaliation for this act on 10 July 1927 by members of the IRA. He and Mary had three children, two girls and a boy who died in infancy. (*Courtesy of Kilmainham Gaol Archives, 20PC-1A45-20*)

Sighle Humphreys was born in 1899 and was the daughter of Nell Humphreys and niece of 'The' O'Rahilly. She joined Cumann na mBan in 1919 and became an organiser stationed in Kerry during the War of Independence. Like the rest of her family Sighle opposed the Treaty. During the Civil War she was O/C of the Ranelagh Branch, Cumann na mBan, and carried out propaganda work for the anti-Treaty IRA. She was arrested after the pro-Treaty forces captured Ernie O'Malley at her mother's home. She took part in the gunfight that broke out while they were trying to arrest O'Malley and was imprisoned in Mountjoy, Kilmainham and the NDU. While imprisoned in Kilmainham she was involved with Judy Gaughran and a number of other women in digging an escape tunnel. Their efforts were in vain when, after a month of digging, the tunnel was discovered by one of the matrons. She was released on 29 November 1923.

Sighle continued in her involvement with Cumann na mBan after her release and over the next ten years was imprisoned many times for her Republican activities. She remained a committed Republican for the rest of her life.

In 1935 she married Donal O'Donoghue, a member of the Dublin Brigade IRA and later a member of the Army Council. They had two children – Dara, who died at birth, and a daughter, Cróine. Sighle died in 1994. She was ninety-five years old. (*Courtesy of Mark Humphrys*)

Madge Clifford was born in Ballybane, Firies, Co. Kerry. She joined the Tralee Branch of Cumann na mBan when it was established in January 1915. Part of her work and that of her colleagues at the time was taking lessons in drill, first aid and sewing classes so that they could make the equipment needed by the Volunteers, for example haversacks and sleeping bags. On Good Friday 1916 the members of the Tralee Branch, including Madge, mobilised and reported for duty at the Tralee Rink, the hall used by the Volunteers, and took care of the Volunteers who were awaiting orders from Dublin.

After the Rising Madge moved to Dublin and became a member of the Central Branch, Cumann na mBan. During the War of Independence she was confidential secretary to Austin Stack, Minister for Home Affairs in the Dáil. She held this position from 1919 until 1922 and worked in Stack's offices located throughout the city including Middle Abbey Street, Molesworth Street and Wellington Quay. Often she carried out her work alone and as the War of Independence escalated and raids by the crown forces became more frequent, women like Madge faced increasing danger. In one such raid by the Auxiliaries on her office in Middle Abbey Street in 1920, Madge, despite being alone, succeeded in hiding important documents from them. She was questioned but used her charm and the raiding party left empty-handed. For many of the women who worked as secretaries, scenes like this were almost part of everyday life.

Madge opposed the Treaty and continued her work as confidential secretary to Stack. When the Civil War began on 28 June 1922, Madge was attached to the anti-Treaty garrison in the Four Courts. When the garrison surrendered on 30 June she escaped and became Ernie O'Malley's secretary and assistant. She held this position from July until O'Malley's arrest at the home of Nell Humphreys in November 1922. During this time Madge accompanied the anti-Treaty IRA to Blessington where she was arrested. She was taken to Portobello Barracks but escaped soon after and resumed her work with Ernie O'Malley.

After O'Malley's arrest Madge moved south to Munster and became secretary to Liam Lynch, commander-in-chief of the anti-Treaty forces, and she held this position until Lynch was killed in action in April 1923. In 1925 Madge married IRA veteran Dr Jack Comer.

Madge Clifford died in Killarney in 1983. She was eighty-eight years old. (*Courtesy of Tim Horgan*)

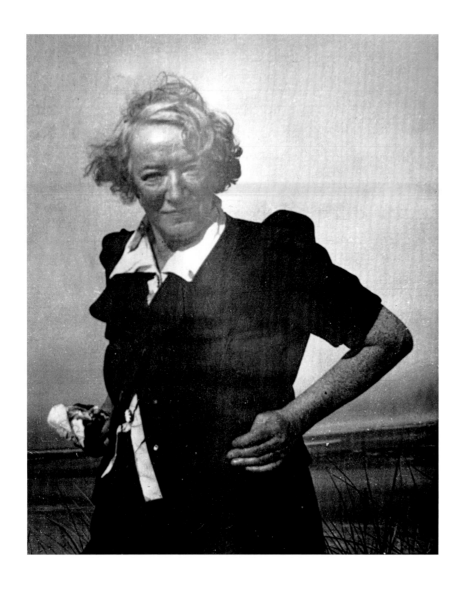

Both the pro- and anti-Treaty factions in the Civil War knew how powerful propaganda could be. But it was the women who utilised it to its full effect, as they had done in the aftermath of the Easter Rising and during the War of Independence. They were the voice of many who could not speak and during the Civil War one of the most powerful weapons the anti-Treaty IRA had at their disposal was their propaganda machine, mainly run by women. They were vitriolic in their attacks on the government and National Army, not just in their bulletins but also in their artwork, the main contributors being Countess Markievicz and Grace Gifford Plunkett (*pictured*). Grace, who had married Joseph Plunkett in Kilmainham Gaol just hours before his execution following the 1916 Rising, was arrested in February 1923. She was imprisoned in Kilmainham Gaol for her activities, as was her sister Catherine. While there she continued to practise her skills, painting numerous murals on the prison walls, most famously the Kilmainham Madonna, which she painted on the back wall of her cell in the East Wing of the gaol. She was released in August 1923 after which she continued to work as an artist. Her works were published in two books. She was a widow for almost forty years and died in 1955, aged sixty-seven. (*Courtesy of Kilmainham Gaol Archives, 21PO-1A51-09*)

Eileen Blackwell, Drumbane, Pallas Green, Limerick, was a member of Cumann na mBan and opposed the Treaty. She was arrested on 4 June 1923 and imprisoned in Kilmainham Gaol. (*Courtesy of Phil Fitzgerald*)

Hannah Clifford, from Clogher, Co. Tipperary, was a teacher and was living in Boherbee, Co. Kerry, at the time of her arrest in 1923. Hannah was imprisoned in Kilmainham Gaol with a number of anti-Treaty women from Kerry. She lost her job as a result of her activities and imprisonment. Upon her release she trained to be a nurse. (*Courtesy of Kilmainham Gaol Archives, 20PC-1B52-15*)

Nora Brosnan was from Castlegregory, Co. Kerry. Like most of her comrades in the Republican movement in Kerry, she opposed the Treaty. She was arrested by pro-Treaty forces in October 1922, when she was only seventeen years old, and was imprisoned in Tralee Gaol, Kilmainham Gaol and the NDU. She was released a year later in October 1923. Nora emigrated to America and married Patrick McKenna, who was a member of the IRA. (*Courtesy of Kilmainham Gaol Archives, 20PC-1A58-09*)

Susie Browne was born in 1901/1902 and lived in Bewley Street, New Ross, Co. Wexford. She was a member of Cumann na mBan. She opposed the Treaty and in 1923, during the Civil War, was arrested and imprisoned in Kilmainham Gaol. She later became a mid-wife and married Thomas Brosnan. She had five children. Susie Browne died in the early 1950s. (*Courtesy of Kilmainham Gaol Archives, 20PC-1B52-03*)

Katherine (Jake) Folan was from Sea Road, Co. Galway. Jake's older sister was active in the anti-Treaty movement in Galway and was known to the authorities. Jake herself was a messenger for the anti-Treaty IRA. In March 1923 pro-Treaty forces came to her home to arrest her sister, who was not there. Rather than leave with no prisoner, they arrested Jake. She was just fifteen years old. Jake was transferred from Galway to Kilmainham Gaol. While there she was involved in the riot that took place on 30 April 1923. She was transferred to the NDU where she was held until her release in September. Jake lived in Dublin for a time before going to America where she found work in the care industry. She returned to Ireland in 1932 and married Tom Savage, a friend from childhood. They moved to London and had a daughter. Jake Folan died in 1989. She was eighty-two. (*Courtesy of Kilmainham Gaol Archives, 20PC-1B52-19*)

Teresa Reddin was in the minority of the members of not just the Cumann na mBan executive but the entire organisation who voted for acceptance of the Treaty. As a result of this she resigned from Cumann na mBan.

The Reddin family firmly supported the Treaty. During the Civil War, in 1923, Teresa's home in Rockfield was burned to the ground by anti-Treaty forces. The family moved to Fitzwilliam Square and Teresa had no more involvement with politics, instead devoting her time to encouraging and promoting Irish culture and the arts. She died in the 1940s. (*Courtesy of Iseult McCarthy*)

At the time of the signing of the Anglo-Irish Treaty, Maud Gonne was in Paris working on behalf of the Republican movement. She initially supported the Treaty and returned to Ireland. In the months leading up to the Civil War she and a number of women worked tirelessly to try to avert the conflict becoming a reality, but when the war began she and her comrades sought instead to help those affected by the conflict. She could not support the Provisional Government when they began executing Republican prisoners in November 1922 and once again threw herself into working on behalf of those in prison, including her son, Seán. She set up the Women's Prisoners' Defence League and they held weekly meetings in Dublin city highlighting what was happening. During the hunger strike of 1923 she and the other members of the League held vigils outside Mountjoy Prison and as a result of her activities Maud was arrested and imprisoned. She went on hunger strike and was released after twenty days. Maud Gonne continued to devote her life to the cause of political prisoners' right up until her death in 1953 at the age of eighty-six. (*Courtesy of Military Archives, Lawlor Collection, PC-59-3-6*)

While the majority of the IRA brigades and Cumann na mBan branches opposed the Treaty, the majority of the ordinary people, the civilians, accepted it, and in most cases the National Army were welcomed into their communities and were assisted by the local population. This help was readily accepted, especially in relation to basic necessities like clothing and food and other home comforts. The Provisional Government was not prepared for the sudden increase in the number of troops it needed to fight the war. In the first few months there were over 20,000 soldiers in the army, and although they had enough weaponry, the government did not have enough in terms of the basics needed to keep that army functioning. (*Courtesy of Military Archives, PC-59-3-6*)

Women assist in first aid for National Army troops. (*Courtesy of Military Archives, PC-59-3-6*)

Margaret Alice O'Brien, or Peg as she was known to her family, was born in Dalkey, Co. Dublin, in 1899. She was a member of Cumann na mBan. Peg opposed the Treaty and was arrested on 17 February 1923 and imprisoned in Kilmainham Gaol. She was released on 14 July 1923, having served 147 days in prison. Peg married John O'Keeffe in 1938. John was a member of the 6th Battalion, Dublin Brigade, IRA, who ran a successful publishing company, James Duffy and Co., specialising in the publication of books relating to all aspects of Irish nationalist and cultural life. Peg later became involved with the Irish Red Cross. John O'Keeffe died in 1987 and Peg died in 1995, aged ninety-six. (*Courtesy of Miriam O'Keeffe and John Brennan*)

Mary Boyce (née Dunne) was from Rutland Street, Dublin, and was a member of the Drumcondra Branch of Cumann na mBan. Her younger brothers, Tom and John, were members of the Volunteers and later the IRA. Tom had fought in North King Street during the Rising. Both fought during the War of Independence and Mary was a courier for the IRA, carrying dispatches and weapons to the various companies, as well as carrying out her other duties for Cumann na mBan. Mary and her brothers opposed the Treaty and her brother Tom fought in the Four Courts at the outbreak of the Civil War.

Mary married Edward Boyce in the early 1920s. Edward was from Foley Street, Dublin and had joined the Volunteers in 1913. He was one of the many thousands to join John Redmond's National Volunteers after the organisation split over Redmond's pledge that the Volunteers would fight for the Allies in Europe. He fought in the war and was wounded in France. (*Courtesy of Ruairi Boyce*)

Florence MacDermott (*back row, far right*) was a member of the Ranelagh Branch, Cumann na mBan, and served under Sighle Humphreys who was O/C of the branch at the time. Florence opposed the Treaty and was arrested during the Civil War and imprisoned in Kilmainham Gaol. She was involved in the 'Kilmainham Riot' which took place on 30 April 1923 as a result of the female political prisoners refusing to leave the gaol for transfer to the NDU. After her release she emigrated to America in 1926 and married John D. McCashin. (*Courtesy of Kilmainham Gaol Archives, 2010.0016*)

Lily Coventry was from Clanbrassil Street, Dublin and was a member of the Éamonn Ceannt Branch, Cumann na mBan. She took the anti-Treaty side in the Civil War, during which time she transported arms for the anti-Treaty IRA. She was arrested for her activities and was imprisoned in Kilmainham Gaol. Upon her release she continued to be politically active and was elected to the executive of Cumann na mBan in October 1923. She married Bill Russell, the brother of Seán Russell, 2nd Battalion, Dublin Brigade, IRA. She and Bill ran a fruit and vegetable shop in Nottingham Street, the North Strand, and they also had a sugar factory in Spring Garden Street, a fairly successful business providing ground down sugar to bakeries all over the country. They also used this business as a cover for storing and transporting weapons for the IRA. Lily was a trustee of An Cumann Cabhrach, the Republican Aid Committee, from 1953. This committee was established to raise funds for the dependants of Republicans in prison at this time. (*Courtesy of Victor Edmonds*)

Rita Farrelly (*pictured*) and her sisters Annie and Kathleen were members of the UCD Branch, Cumann na mBan. Rita was imprisoned in Mountjoy Prison during the War of Independence and again during the Civil War, which is where she met her future husband, Patrick Fleming (*right*), who was also a prisoner in Mountjoy at the time. Patrick was from The Swan in Co. Laois and was a member of the IRA. His brother Éamonn was O/C of the Laois Volunteers in 1916. The brothers took opposing sides during the Civil War, Éamonn supporting the Treaty while Patrick and Rita opposed it. Rita was transferred to Kilmainham Gaol during the Civil War and was involved in the riot that took place on 30 April 1923. Rita, with Brighid O'Mullane, was the first to be forcibly removed from the top floor landing of the East Wing. It took the authorities five hours to remove sixty-five women from the wing. Rita and Patrick married in 1925 and had five children. (*Courtesy of Jim Fleming*)

Catalina Bulfin was born in Buenos Aires in 1900. Her parents, William and Annie, were Irish and returned to Ireland in 1902, settling in Birr, Co. Offaly. Her brother Éamonn was a pupil at St Enda's school, Rathfarnham, Dublin. Some time around 1920 Catalina moved to Dublin and became involved in the nationalist movement. She worked for Austin Stack when he was Minister for Home Affairs during the War of Independence. Catalina opposed the Treaty. She was arrested on 6 April 1923 in Stack's office and was imprisoned in Kilmainham Gaol and the NDU. She was released in October 1923.

Catalina married Seán MacBride, son of Maud Gonne and John MacBride, in 1926. However, it was a while before the young couple would settle into married life, for Seán, who had opposed the Treaty and was a senior member of the IRA, was on the run and between 1927 and 1929 was arrested and imprisoned at least twice. They lived in Roebuck House, Clonskeagh with Seán's mother and the role of provider fell to Catalina, a role that many women had to fill during the years of the conflict. She was employed in the Hospital Sweepstakes lottery set up to raise money to finance hospitals around the country. Catalina and Seán had two children, Anna and Tiernan. Catalina died in 1976, aged seventy-six. (*Courtesy of Kilmainham Gaol Archives, 20PC-1B52-11*)

As the Civil War progressed raids by Free State forces became more frequent. Áine Ceannt's home in Ranelagh was raided three times and during one particularly brutal raid in February 1923 Free State troops proceeded to destroy her home, as can be seen in these photographs. The saddest thing according to Áine regarding this raid in particular was the fact that despite all the raids she had endured by the military and Auxiliaries during the War of Independence they did not destroy her property and her belongings. She was most upset by the destruction of a photograph of her husband Éamonn, seen in the foreground of the photograph above. (*Courtesy of the National Library of Ireland*)

Judy Gaughran was from Dunmahon, Co. Louth. She moved to Dublin and joined the Fairview Branch, Cumann na mBan after the Rising. She later became captain of the branch. Judy opposed the Treaty and during the Civil War she was acting as adjutant to the 2nd Battalion, Dublin Brigade, anti-Treaty IRA. She was arrested in October 1922 and was imprisoned in Kilmainham Gaol and the NDU. During her imprisonment in Kilmainham, Judy was involved in digging an escape tunnel in the basement laundry in the old West Wing. The women worked tirelessly for a month, digging away while their comrades created distractions for them to do their work. The tunnel was discovered but the women were not disheartened. Judy was a member of the prisoners' council in the NDU.

She married Ned O'Reilly who was a member of the 3rd Tipperary Brigade. They had met during the War of Independence while he was a prisoner in Limerick Gaol. They went to America in 1927 but later returned to Ireland, settling in Clanalty, near Cashel, Co. Tipperary. They had three children, one boy and two girls. (*Courtesy of Kilmainham Gaol Archives, 20PC-1B55-04*)

Christina (Chriss) Behan was born in 1903 and lived in Hackett's Court, Kevin Street, Dublin and worked in Jacob's Biscuit Factory. She was a member of the Clan na nGaedheal Girl Scouts and is seen wearing their uniform aged about seventeen in this photograph. She opposed the Treaty. As the Civil War escalated anyone suspected of being a member of any anti-Treaty organisation could be arrested and on 16 March 1923 Chriss was arrested for being a member of Clan na nGaedheal. She was taken to Kilmainham Gaol and later transferred to the NDU. On 4 July Chriss went on hunger strike with two other women, Jenny Lynch and May Whelan, in protest at their treatment in the NDU. They were released after eleven days on hunger strike. Upon her release Chriss married and had a family, seven girls and one boy. In later life she rarely spoke of the part that she played in the Irish revolution but she remained proud of her involvement and when Kilmainham Gaol opened as a museum in 1966 she returned, this time as a guest. Chriss Behan died in 1995. She was ninety-two. (*Courtesy of Doreen Behan*)

Nellie Fennell was born in 1893. She was arrested during the Civil War and imprisoned in Kilmainham Gaol and the NDU. Nellie died in 1928. She was only thirty-three years old. (*Courtesy of Kilmainham Gaol Archives, 2010.0197*)

Above left: Nellie Merrigan.

Above right: Nellie Merrigan (*left*) and Kathleen Kavanagh (*right*).

Nellie Merrigan and Kathleen Kavanagh were sisters-in-law, Kathleen having married Nellie's brother Tom. Both women were members of the Colmcille Branch, Cumann na mBan. Kathleen, Nellie and her sister Lizzie took the anti-Treaty side during the Civil War. Nellie and Lizzie were arrested in Jacob's Biscuit Factory by Nellie's former fiancé, a National Army soldier, on 12 March 1923. Nellie was imprisoned in Kilmainham Gaol and not released until 6 October 1923. She died in 1989, aged ninety-one.

Kathleen remained an active Republican after her release from prison and in 1931 she joined Saor Éire which had been set up by veteran IRA men who did not approve of the conservative Republicanism that was being promoted. This group, along with other Republican organisations including Cumann na mBan, were proscribed and Kathleen was once again arrested for being a member of the organisation. She had by then been elected onto the executive of Cumann na mBan. (*Courtesy of Kilmainham Gaol Archives, 18PO-1B53-17*)

Elizabeth Maguire, from Phibsboro in Dublin, joined the Drumcondra Branch of Cumann na mBan in January 1918 and helped in the Sinn Féin campaign for the general election that year. She also worked collecting for the Prisoners' Dependants' Fund and during the War of Independence was a dispatch carrier for the IRA. Her brother, Tom, was a member of the 5th Battalion Engineers, Dublin Brigade, IRA.

Elizabeth opposed the Treaty and when the Civil War broke out she was on active service in O'Connell Street, Capel Street, Blessington Street and Ormond Quay, carrying dispatches and gathering intelligence on troop movements. Her house was used by the anti-Treaty IRA for assembling detonators and she also assisted in the escape of a Republican prisoner from Beggars Bush Barracks, whom she kept hidden in her home for a number of weeks. Tom also took the anti-Treaty side during the Civil War and was killed with three other anti-Treaty IRA men on 18 November 1922, when the mine they were transporting prematurely exploded. He was twenty-two years old.

Elizabeth married Daniel O'Driscoll in the mid-1920s. Daniel, originally from Schull, Co. Cork, was a member of 'C' Company, 4th Battalion, Cork No. 1 Brigade, IRA. He moved to Dublin in 1920 and joined the 5th Battalion Engineers, Dublin Brigade, where he would have met Elizabeth's brother Tom. Daniel fought on the anti-Treaty side during the Civil War in Moran's Hotel, Talbot Street and was arrested and imprisoned for his activities. (*Courtesy of Richard O'Driscoll and Mick Doyle*)

Francis 'Fanny' Kelly was born on 22 April 1887 in Rathmoyle, Abbeyleix, Co. Laois and was the youngest of eleven children born to Patrick and Bridget Kelly. Her father had been a member of the Land League and was imprisoned in Mountjoy Prison for five years during the Land War in the 1880s for promoting the use of boycotting against the local landlords. Coming from such a political background it was no surprise that Fanny became involved in the Republican movement.

Fanny joined Cumann na mBan when a branch was established in Abbeyleix in the aftermath of the Rising. Throughout the War of Independence she made parcels of food and other home comforts for local IRA men imprisoned in Maryborough, Kildare, Kilkenny and Mountjoy Prisons.

Fanny opposed the Treaty and on 20 March 1923 she was arrested by pro-Treaty forces at her home in Abbeyleix. She resisted arrest and had to be forcibly removed, being dragged down the garden path by the soldiers. She was taken to Portobello Barracks and then to Kilmainham Gaol. Fanny immediately went on hunger strike in protest at her treatment. Her strike lasted seven days after which she was allowed to receive parcels of food and other basic essentials from home.

On 30 April Fanny was one of the many women involved in the 'Kilmainham Riot', which took place as a result of the women's refusal to be transferred to the NDU. They had to be forcibly removed from the gaol by Free State troops and many of the women were injured in this incident. Fanny was dragged down the main staircase in the Gaol's East Wing by five men alone.

While in the NDU Fanny was involved in the attempted escape in which the women dug a tunnel, but before they could complete it their plan was discovered. In September 1923 Fanny was released and she returned home to Abbeyleix.

After the Civil War Fanny found work as a Home Assistance Officer for the No. 2 District of the Laois County Board of Health. She married Joseph Lalor in July 1925 and they had one child, a son, Patrick, who was born in 1926. Fanny and Joe later opened a grocery shop in Abbeyleix. Fanny Kelly died on 17 December 1944. She was fifty-seven years old. (*Courtesy of Paddy Lalor and Veronica Daly*)

Marcella (*left*) and Ellen Murphy were from Brideswell, Gorey, Co. Wexford. Marcella was born in 1889 and Ellen in 1890. They were childhood friends of Máire Deegan who was a member of Cumann na mBan. With their brother Patrick, Marcella and Ellen became involved in the Republican movement. Patrick joined the 5th Battalion, North Wexford Brigade, IRA, and Marcella and Ellen were members of the Gorey Branch, 4th North Wexford Cumann na mBan.

During the War of Independence their family home in Brideswell was used as a safe house by the local IRA. In time they came to the attention of the Black and Tans who raided the house on a regular basis looking for their brother.

Marcella, Ellen and Patrick opposed the Treaty and when the Civil War began the women continued to provide their house as a hideout for anti-Treaty IRA men. Known for their Republican sympathies, their house was raided on a number of occasions by pro-Treaty forces and in one such raid a number of anti-Treaty IRA men were arrested. Their brother Patrick was sent to the Curragh internment camp. Despite the fact that they were known to be sheltering the men, neither Marcella nor Ellen was arrested.

Neither sister married. Marcella cared for her elderly mother at the family home while after the revolution Ellen moved to Dublin to help rear her sister Kate's children, after which she returned to Brideswell. Marcella died in 1974, aged eighty-five. Ellen died in 1983. She was ninety-three years old. (*Courtesy of Marcella Byrne*)

Caitlín Brugha (née Kingston) was born in Birr, Co. Offaly, in 1879. She married Cathal Brugha in 1912 and they had six children, five girls and one boy. They met while Cathal was attending an Irish class in Birr. Cathal was elected as a TD for Waterford during the 1918 general election and after he was killed in the Civil War, Caitlín ran for election for his seat. She was elected as TD to Waterford in 1923. In 1924 she set up a drapery business, Kingston's Ltd, with premises on O'Connell Street, right on the site known as 'The Block' where her husband had fought and was fatally wounded in July 1922. In June 1927 Caitlín was re-elected but did not take her seat in the Dáil. She refused to join de Valera when he formed Fianna Fáil. Caitlín Brugha was a committed Republican all her life. She died in December 1959 at eighty years of age. (*Courtesy of Waterford County Museum, UK 2908*)

Members of Cumann na mBan stand over Liam Lynch's grave, Fermoy, Co. Cork. Liam Lynch was killed in the Knockmealdown mountains, Tipperary, in April 1923. Cumann na mBan provided an honour guard at his funeral, members of which are shown here. With his death, de Valera and Frank Aiken, Lynch's successor as chief of staff of the anti-Treaty forces, ordered the Republicans to lay down their arms. Less than a month later, in May 1923, the Civil War was over. (*Courtesy of Waterford County Museum, UK 2901*)

Miss Barry O'Delany, Maud Gonne and Annie MacSwiney stand vigil outside Mountjoy Prison in protest at the imprisonment by the Free State authorities of Annie's sister Mary and other Republicans, November 1922. Annie refused to leave the prison and began a hunger strike. After eleven days on hunger strike outside the prison she was herself arrested and imprisoned. She was soon released, but in February 1923 she was again arrested for her refusal to stop her vigil outside the prisons and was held in Kilmainham Gaol. Although the Civil War ended in May 1923, the Free State government was reluctant to release those who had fought against it. In all over 16,000 men and women were interned in prisons all over the country. In response to this the Republicans began a hunger strike in protest at the imprisonment, which included both the men and the women. On the outside women such as Maud Gonne continued to highlight the plight of those imprisoned through marches and demonstrations. The government refused to grant a general amnesty and refused to back down. They knew how powerful a tool the hunger strike could be but they stood firm. The strike was eventually called off and soon, little by little, the releases began. (*Courtesy of Mercier Archive*)

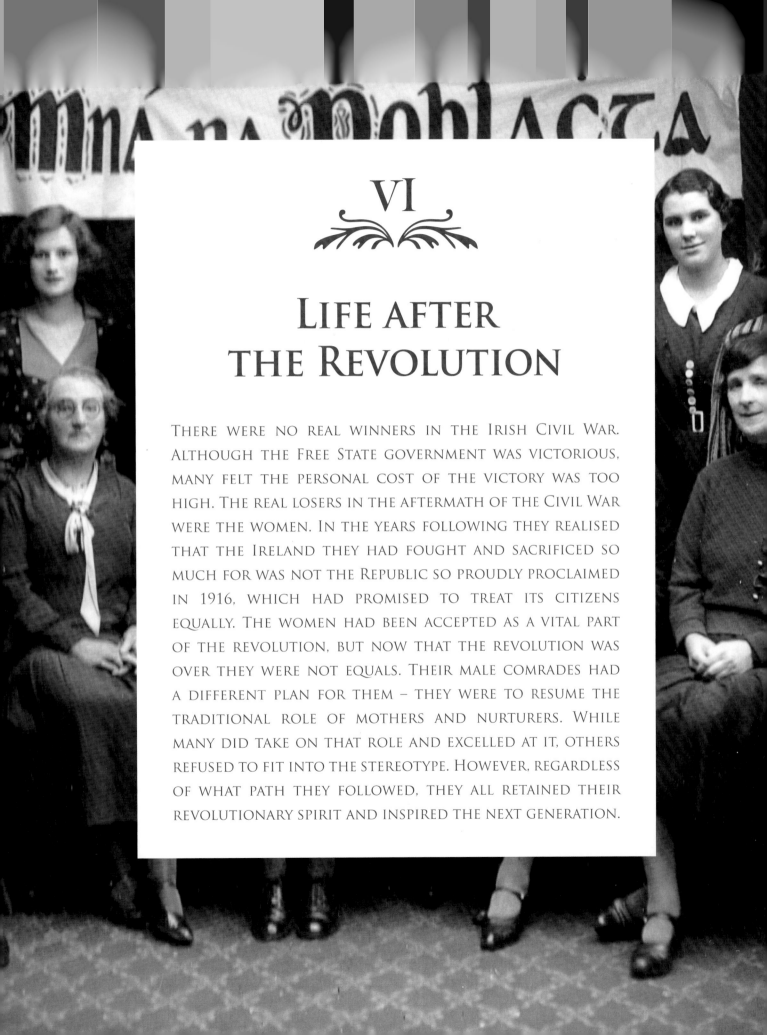

VI

Life after the Revolution

There were no real winners in the Irish Civil War. Although the Free State government was victorious, many felt the personal cost of the victory was too high. The real losers in the aftermath of the Civil War were the women. In the years following they realised that the Ireland they had fought and sacrificed so much for was not the Republic so proudly proclaimed in 1916, which had promised to treat its citizens equally. The women had been accepted as a vital part of the revolution, but now that the revolution was over they were not equals. Their male comrades had a different plan for them – they were to resume the traditional role of mothers and nurturers. While many did take on that role and excelled at it, others refused to fit into the stereotype. However, regardless of what path they followed, they all retained their revolutionary spirit and inspired the next generation.

When the Civil War began on 28 June Countess Markievicz presented herself for duty with the anti-Treaty forces at Barry's Hotel and later fought in the Hammam Hotel on O'Connell Street. After the fall of Dublin she evaded arrest and carried out propaganda work for the Republicans, going to Scotland to campaign on behalf of the Republican movement. She returned to Ireland after the Civil War ended in May 1923 and in the general election that year won back her seat in Dáil Éireann but refused to attend. While campaigning for the release of anti-Treaty prisoners she was arrested by pro-Treaty forces. While being held in the NDU she went on hunger strike. She was released on Christmas Eve 1923 having spent four weeks in prison.

In March 1926 Éamon de Valera resigned from Sinn Féin and formed Fianna Fáil. In the general election of June 1927 Fianna Fáil nominated eighty-seven candidates, winning forty-four seats. Countess Markievicz joined Fianna Fáil and was elected, but never took her seat. Her health had been in decline in recent years and while in hospital having an operation on her appendix she developed peritonitis. She died in Sir Patrick Dunn's Hospital, Dublin, on 15 July 1927. She was fifty-nine years old.

Her remains were taken to St Andrew's church, Westland Row, after which she was moved to the Rotunda Hospital where she lay in state, her remains visited by thousands of the working class and poor people of the inner city to whom she had dedicated her life in the preceding years. Éamon de Valera helped carry her coffin and delivered the graveside oration. She is buried in Glasnevin Cemetery. (*Courtesy of Martin O'Dwyer*)

Mrs Margaret Pearse starting the machinery for the printing of the first issue of the *Irish Press*, 5 September 1931. The *Irish Press* was set up by Éamon de Valera as an independent newspaper that was not affiliated to any political party. It was set up with money raised during the lecture tours of America by the Republican movement during the War of Independence. The paper ran for sixty-four years, ceasing publication in May 1995. At its peak the paper boasted a readership of 200,000 people.

Margaret Pearse died less than a year after this photograph was taken, in April 1932. She was seventy-four years old. (*Courtesy of the Pearse Museum, 2004.0197*)

Dr Kathleen Lynn was a true radical throughout her life. During the Easter Rising she was Chief Medical Officer in the ICA and served with the City Hall garrison. After the surrender she was imprisoned in Richmond Barracks, Kilmainham Gaol and Mountjoy Prison, before being deported to England and placed in the care of Dr Cusack in Bath, where she assisted him in his doctor's practice. She returned to Ireland in August 1916.

In 1917 Kathleen became a member of the Sinn Féin executive and after the 'German Plot' arrests in 1918 went on the run. Although arrested, she was soon released as this was at the height of the Spanish Flu epidemic and qualified doctors were needed to treat the sick.

At this time Dublin city had the highest rate of infant mortality in Europe. Determined to address this, Kathleen, with Madeleine Ffrench-Mullen and a committee of dedicated women, set up St Ultan's Infant Hospital in Charlemont Street, Dublin. It opened its doors on Ascension Thursday 1919.

With the establishment of Dáil Éireann in January 1919, Kathleen was appointed Director of Public Health. In 1920 she was elected to Rathmines Council. Kathleen served on the Public Health Committee, the Housing Committee and the Milk Committee of the Council. She was also a member of the Irish White Cross. Throughout the War of Independence, her home on Belgrave Road, Dublin, was regularly raided by the authorities.

Kathleen opposed the Treaty and in May 1922 she assisted anti-Treaty forces with first aid in Waterford. During the Civil War both her home and St Ultan's were raided by pro-Treaty forces. In the general election in August 1923 Kathleen stood for Sinn Féin and she won a seat in Dublin North, but she refused to take her seat in the Dáil. She opposed de Valera's proposal to enter the Dáil in 1926. That same year she and Ffrench-Mullen focused their attention on addressing the social issues affecting the ordinary people, and they put forward proposals to the government concerning housing, education and food schemes for children. Like many of her comrades Kathleen opposed the 1937 Constitution.

Kathleen Lynn was always looking for ways to improve the health and wellbeing of the children of Ireland and she introduced the widespread use of the BCG vaccine in Ireland. She was also a supporter of the teachings of Dr Maria Montessori and her approach to children's welfare. In 1934 Montessori visited St Ultan's. Kathleen Lynn died in 1955. She was eighty-one years old. (*Courtesy of Kilmainham Gaol Archives, 17PO-IB52-13*)

Towards the end of the Civil War Kathleen Clarke opened a shop in D'Olier Street, Dublin. She was arrested by the Free State authorities in April 1923 while trying to arrange a meeting between de Valera and a journalist who wished to interview him. She was taken to Kilmainham Gaol but was only held for one night. Kathleen continued to work with the INAAVDF and in 1924 she undertook a trip to America to raise money for the organisation. She was a founder member of Fianna Fáil in 1926 and was elected to the Senate serving between 1928 and 1936 until the Senate was abolished. She vehemently opposed the Conditions of Employment Bill of 1935, which was to set the women's rights movement in Ireland back years. It was claimed that this bill would protect the jobs of men who, it was believed, were being overlooked in favour of women. When Kathleen demanded to know just what jobs the women were taking from the men, she did not get a reply. She also opposed the 1937 Constitution, specifically the articles limiting the rights of women.

In 1939 Kathleen became the first lady lord mayor of Dublin. One of the first things she did was to remove all the portraits of the British monarchs which had hung in the Mansion House. During her time as lord mayor she helped set up the Irish Red Cross, of which she was elected president. She served as lord mayor until 1941 when she resigned from the Fianna Fáil party due to differences of opinion. In 1947 she joined Clann na Poblachta, a Republican party with ideas of social reform set up by Seán MacBride.

At this time Kathleen was also a board member for a number of institutions and organisations, including St Ultan's Infant Hospital, Grangegorman Mental Hospital and the Rotunda Maternity Hospital, and she was also a member of the executive committee of Holles Street Maternity Hospital. She was involved in the City of Dublin Vocational Education Committee, the City of Dublin Old Age Pensions Committee, the City of Dublin Child Welfare Committee and the National Monuments Committee, to name a few.

In 1965 Kathleen moved to Liverpool to live with her son Emmet. She returned to Ireland in 1967 to open an exhibition on the Fenians that was held in Kilmainham Gaol.

Kathleen Clarke died in 1972. She was ninety-four years old. (*Courtesy of Kilmainham Gaol Archives, 21PC-3K11-01(4)*)

In 1929 Linda Kearns married Charles Wilson McWhinney. McWhinney had been O/C of the Derry Brigade IRA during the War of Independence and in 1924 he came to Dublin. He stayed with Linda's sister Annie in her home in Gardiner Place and that is most likely how he and Linda met. They had one daughter Ann, born in 1930 (*shown here with her mother*). Linda continued to be politically active; she was a founding member of Fianna Fáil and was elected to the party's executive. She was also a member of the General Nursing Council Committee and the Irish Red Cross. Linda opposed the Conditions of Employment Bill introduced by Fianna Fáil, which was a regressive act against women in the workplace. Linda became a senator in 1938 and was also founder of the Women's Industrial Development Association. She also found time to become secretary of the Irish Nurses' Association. In 1946 Linda set up the Kilrock Nurses' Convalescent and Holiday Home, Howth, Co. Dublin. In 1951 she was presented with the Florence Nightingale Medal for her work in the nursing profession. She died a few weeks later, on 5 June. She was sixty-five years old. (*Courtesy of Delia McDevitt*)

Mary Ellen (*left*) and Margaret Murphy (*right*) were from Carricknagavna, Forkhill, Armagh. Mary Ellen was born in December 1893 and Margaret in December 1897. They were both members of Cumann na mBan in South Armagh, having been introduced to the movement by Nano Aiken, whose brother Frank was O/C of the 4th Northern Division IRA and later chief of staff of the anti-Treaty IRA after the death of Liam Lynch during the Civil War. In 1925 Mary Ellen married William McGuigan, whom she met during the War of Independence when he was stationed with the RIC in Cullyhanna Barracks, South Armagh. He was asked by Michael Collins to transfer to the RUC upon its inception and although a Catholic he was successful in becoming a member. After they were married William was stationed in Benburb, Co. Armagh, Coagh, Co. Tyrone and Springfield Road, Belfast. Although his job required him to arrest people, Mary Ellen forbade him from arresting Republicans and poitín makers! Mary Ellen died in November 1974 and is buried in Milltown Cemetery, Belfast. William died in 1967. Today her house, No. 359 Springfield Road, is no longer there. It is a pillar in the 'Peace Line'.

Margaret Murphy married John Boyle, a fellow Republican from Whitecross, Armagh in 1924. She died in April 1982 and is buried in Tullyherron, Co. Armagh. (*Courtesy of Kevin and Maureen Murphy*)

In 1926 Eileen Bell married Thomas Glynn, who was originally from Scotland. They moved to Scotland in 1929 and spent ten years there. The photo above shows Eileen with her family there in 1937 (*left to right*): Eileen, Aileen, Seamus, Tommy and Thomas. In 1939 they returned to Ireland at the outbreak of the Second World War. In total she had five children, three boys and two girls. The family first lived in Rathmines Road, Dublin before finally settling in Galtimore Road, Drimnagh, Dublin, where Eileen's good friend and fellow member of the Drumcondra Branch, Cumann na mBan, Mary Boyce also lived with her family. The two women remained close friends all their lives. (*Courtesy of Aileen Murray and Anne May*)

Mary Boyce, seen here with her son Éamonn, Jimmy Magill and Ned Groome, was a committed Republican for the rest of her life and continued to support the IRA during the Border Campaign of the 1950s. Her son Éamonn joined the IRA and in the 1950s he was arrested and sentenced to twelve years in prison in Crumlin Road Gaol, Belfast, for leading a raid for arms in Omagh. During his imprisonment Mary's home in Galtimore Road, Drimnagh, was a safe house for IRA men on the run or those recently released from prison; the house was also a dump for arms and explosives. This photograph shows Éamonn after his release from prison in 1962, having served eight years in Crumlin Road. (*Courtesy of Ruairi Boyce*)

Leslie and Tom Barry settled in Cork and during the Second World War, Leslie organised care for children orphaned by the war. She became chairman of the Irish Red Cross and set up the 'Freedom from Hunger' campaign, later known as Gorta, of which she became president. She helped set up the VHI and did great work on behalf of women and those with mental health issues. She received the Henri Dumant medal from the International Committee of the Red Cross in 1978. She died in 1984, aged ninety-one, and is buried in St Finbarr's Cemetery, Cork, beside her husband Tom. (*Courtesy of James Langton*)

After the Civil War many of those who had taken the anti-Treaty side found it very hard to find work. In response to this Charlotte Despard established the Roebuck Jam factory, which unfortunately proved unsuccessful. She remained a committed Republican, socialist and advocate of the working class, and set up the Irish Workers' College in Eccles Street, Dublin in 1933. Never one to ignore a challenge, she moved to Belfast in the mid-1930s to try and unite the Catholic and Protestant working class. She died on 9 November 1939. She was ninety-five years old. (*Courtesy of Kilmainham Gaol Archives, 19PO-1A32-21a*)

The Irish White Cross was set up in December 1920 in Dublin in order to raise money to aid those suffering as a result of the War of Independence, especially those who had loved ones in prison or who had lost their businesses or homes due to reprisals carried out by the crown forces. Amongst those on the council were Áine Ceannt (*right*), who was also a founding member, Kathleen Clarke (*left*), Máire Comerford and Nancy O'Rahilly (*second right*). In America 'The American Committee for Relief in Ireland' was established and, along with donors from Canada, this organisation was successful in raising £1,281,906 0s 4d. In total donations around the world raised £1,371,284 11s 7d for the Irish White Cross. This money was used not only to rebuild homes and businesses but also provide relief to the widows of IRA men who had been killed and children whose parents were in prison or had been killed, as well as those wounded during the conflict, paying for artificial limbs where possible. For many this money was a lifeline. Áine Ceannt was secretary to the Irish White Cross Children's Relief Association from 1922 until 1947, when the White Cross finally closed its doors. This section specifically looked after the children affected by the conflict. (*Courtesy of Kilmainham Gaol Archives, 21PC-1K42-18*)

Éamonn Ceannt Cumann, Sinn Féin, on a group trip to Glendalough, 19 July 1931. Back row fifth from left is Lil Coventry, fourth and fifth from right are Lar and May Farrell. Second row third from right is Bobby O'Brien. First row second from right is Connie O'Brien. Both Lar Farrell and Bobby O'Brien were members of the IRA, while Lar's wife May and her sister Connie were members of Cumann na mBan during the War of Independence and Civil War. (*Courtesy of Lorcan Collins*)

Members of the Fairview Branch, Cumann na mBan at an engagement at Áras an Uachtaráin hosted by President Seán T. O'Kelly and his wife Phyllis Ryan, 1946. Amongst those in the photograph are Sarah Kealy (*back row, first left*), Amee (May) Wisely (*back row, second from right*), Jenny Nugent (née Colley) (*back row, far right*), Tilly Simpson (*front row, third left*) and Gertie Colley (*front row, fourth left*).

Gertie Colley, Sarah Kealy and May Wisely all took part in the Easter Rising, based with the GPO, Jacob's Biscuit Factory and St Stephen's Green/College of Surgeons garrisons respectively. During the War of Independence Colley and Kealy used their homes as safe houses for Volunteers on the run, while Wisely used her mother's home in Clontarf to hide men arms and ammunition. Although Kealy and Wisely took no part in the Civil War, Gertie Colley was attached to the anti-Treaty IRA garrison in Barry's Hotel, Gardiner's Row, Dublin. She evaded arrest after the main battle in Dublin ended and continued to work for the Republicans. She was given control of the money owned by the anti-Treaty and was also a courier for Frank Henderson, O/C anti-Treaty IRA, Dublin Brigade. (*Courtesy of Kilmainham Gaol Archives, 17MS-1B52-18*)

Mná na Phoblachta in the 1930s. At the Cumann na mBan Convention in 1933 it was proposed to change their constitution so that the Oath of Allegiance to the first and second Dáil be removed. They wished to remain loyal to the Irish Republic proclaimed in 1916 and to support a Republican government representing the whole country. As a result of this change a number of women, including many who had been founding members of Cumann na mBan left the organisation, including Mary MacSwiney, Elizabeth O'Farrell and Julia Grenan. In September 1933 a meeting was held by these women with the aim of setting up a new organisation and in November of that year Mná na Phoblachta was established and pledged in its constitution to remain loyal to Dáil Éireann, the legitimate government of the Republic. Standing (*left to right*): — Allen, Josie McDonnell, Frances Tubbert, Amy Langan, Nodlag Brugha, May Murray, Kathleen O'Higgins, Bridh Kelly, Noinín Brugha and Lily Anderson. Seated: Eileen Tubbert, Mrs O'Moore, Julia Grenan, Mrs Shelley and Miss O'Carroll. May Murray, Eileen Tubbert and Mrs O'Moore had been imprisoned in Kilmainham Gaol during the Civil War. Julia Grenan had been imprisoned in Kilmainham Gaol for her part in the Easter Rising. (*Courtesy of Kilmainham Gaol Archives, 21PO-1B53-28*)

1916–21 Club dinner. The effect of the Civil War was to stay with the people for many years, and is still felt to this day. Despite that, there were a number of organisations which tried to heal the divide, including the 1916–21 Club. It sought to bring together those who had once been enemies, and organisations such as this succeeded in a small way. Annual dinners, like the one seen here, were held, in which both sides of the divide participated. The road to recovery was a long one to travel but through the 1916–21 Club, the GAA and the restoration of Kilmainham Gaol, these people took a small step that in the end turned out to reap huge dividends, as slowly both sides came together. Included in this photograph are Eamon Martin (*left*), Miss Margaret Pearse (*fourth from left*) and Nora Connolly O'Brien (*sixth from left*). (*Courtesy of Eamon Murphy*)

Members of Cumann na mBan attend a reunion event at Áras an Uachtaráin, 23–24 June 1946. This reunion was organised by Phyllis Ryan, wife of President Seán T. O'Kelly, and was one of the events which sought to reunite old comrades. The reunion was open to all members of Cumann na mBan regardless of what side they had taken in the Civil War and was deemed to be a success as women who had taken opposing sides attended the event. (*Courtesy of Bernadine and Audrey Flanagan*)

Reunion of the Drumcondra Branch of Cumann na mBan in the Gresham Hotel, Dublin, in the 1940s. In the aftermath of the Irish revolution, for many men and women the next stage of their life was that of husband, wife, mother and father, and although domestic life was now their priority, many kept in contact with the friends and comrades with whom they had experienced so much during those years. In the 1930s, 1940s, 1950s and 1960s annual dinners were held by individual IRA companies and branches of Cumann na mBan. The general manager in the Gresham Hotel at this time was Timothy 'Toddy' O'Sullivan, who upon discovering just who these ladies were, held their reunion free of charge. Toddy's Bar at the Gresham Hotel is named after O'Sullivan. In this photograph, amongst others are Rose Fitzpatrick (née Mulligan) (*back row, middle*), anti-Treaty, who was imprisoned in Kilmainham Gaol during the Civil War; Mary Boyce (née Dunne) (*front row, second left*), anti-Treaty, who organised many of these reunion dinners; and Annie Burke (*front row, far right*), North Summer Street, Dublin, who came from a well-known Republican family and during a raid on her home by the crown forces during the War of Independence was arrested and held for a number of days. The experience traumatised her so much she never completely recovered from her ordeal. (*Courtesy of Ruairi Boyce*)

Members of Cumann na mBan reminiscing about their many experiences during the revolution at one of their annual dinners at the Gresham Hotel. First left is Teresa Lane (née McDowell), who was a captain of the Fairview Branch. Second left is Elizabeth O'Driscoll, Drumcondra Branch. First standing is Rose Fitzpatrick (née Mulligan) and second standing is Josephine Lyons (née McDowell), both Drumcondra Branch. (*Courtesy of Mick Doyle and Richard O'Driscoll*)

Dolly Lawlor at the Easter Rising commemorations in 1966/67. Dolly is wearing the three medals she received for her service to the Irish revolution. She wears her 1916 medal and 1916 survivor's medal, as well as her Black and Tan medal. Dolly died in 1968. She was sixty-nine years old. (*Courtesy of Bernadine and Audrey Flanagan*)

Bridget 'Cissie' O'Connor was originally from Glasgow and was a member of the Glasgow Branch of Cumann na mBan. During the Civil War she came to Ireland and, while there, she met and fell in love with Seán Scanlan who was a member of the anti-Treaty IRA. They later married and had a daughter Nuala. Here you see the family on Nuala's wedding day. (*Courtesy of Derek Scanlan*)

Mary Slater from the Ivy Buildings, Dublin, was another member of Cumann na mBan who relished her role as a mother after the war. She is seen here at her daughter's wedding. However, she also remained active in the Republican movement up to the 1940s, hiding weapons for the IRA in her home. (*Courtesy of Mark Moloney*)

Survivors of the ICA 1916, taken at Liberty Hall in 1966, with the table on which the Proclamation was signed in 1916 in front of them (*above*), and outside Liberty Hall (*right*) with Rosie Hackett (*centre*) and Frank Robbins (*far right*). Although it may seem like the ICA was defunct after the Rising, this was not the case. Many members refused to join the IRA and retained membership of the ICA, contributing fully in the War of Independence and Civil War. The organisation remained in existence until the 1940s. (*Internal image courtesy of Kilmainham Gaol Archives, 21PO-1A36-05, external image courtesy of Eamon Murphy*)

Mary Breen O'Dwyer, centre, captain of 2nd Battalion, 3rd Tipperary Brigade, Cumann na mBan, having received a civic reception in the council offices, Cashel on her 100th birthday. (*Courtesy of Martin O'Dwyer*)

Margaret Duggan and John Buckley, Mitchell Street, Dungarvan, Co. Waterford, 1968. John was a member of the anti-Treaty IRA and during the Civil War, as in the War of Independence, the IRA depended on the help and support of the local community. Buckley was wanted by the pro-Treaty forces and Margaret helped him elude his pursuers, organising his escape to America. (*Courtesy of Waterford County Museum, TT 493*)

Left to right: Frank Aiken, Linda Kearns, Éamon de Valera, Miss Margaret Pearse and Oscar Traynor. The Pearse family struggled to keep St Enda's school open, but it eventually closed its doors in 1935. Margaret Pearse was elected to the Dáil in 1933 as a Fianna Fáil TD and later entered the Seanad where she was a member until her death in 1968. Patrick Pearse's other sister, Mary Brigid, died in 1947. (*Courtesy of Delia McDevitt*)

Left to right: Thomas Merrigan, Mary Brigid Kavanagh and Kathleen Merrigan (née Kavanagh). Mary Brigid was Kathleen's mother. Kathleen was great friends with Tom's sisters Lizzie and Nellie Merrigan as they had all been members of the Colmcille Branch, Cumann na mBan. Both Thomas and Kathleen took the anti-Treaty side during the Civil War and both were imprisoned for their activities. (*Courtesy of Kilmainham Gaol Archives, 2011.0262*)

Left to right: Nellie Merrigan, Susan Ryan and Thomas Merrigan in later life. Susan Ryan (1884–1965) was the half-sister of Nellie and Thomas. Both Nellie and Susan were members of Colmcille Branch, Cumann na mBan and were both arrested and imprisoned during the Civil War as was Thomas and their younger sister Lizzie, who died in 1926, aged twenty-four. (*Courtesy of Kilmainham Gaol Archives, 2011.0261*)

Mrs May Gibney O'Neill (*left*) and Mrs Essie Purcell (née Snoddy) in Toddy's Lounge, Tullow Street, Carlow, 1981. May and Essie were imprisoned together in Kilmainham Gaol in 1923 during the Civil War for their anti-Treaty activities. May was a veteran of the Easter Rising, having served in the GPO during the fighting. She later married Laurence O'Neill, a member of the Carlow IRA. They met when May was sent to Carlow on behalf of Cumann na mBan during the War of Independence. Essie was also from Carlow and was only sixteen years old when she was imprisoned. After they were released from prison the two women lost contact, got married and had young families and as the years passed both thought the other had died. It was by pure chance that May Gibney discovered her friend was alive and well. May had gone to the National Museum to amend her name on the 1916 roll of honour, as she wanted to include her maiden name, and asked the curator of the Irish history section, Pádraig Ó Snodaigh, if he knew a woman called Essie Snoddy. The two friends were eventually reunited, fifty-eight years after they had last seen each other. In 1923 they were both young women who helped change the course of Irish history. In 1981 they were no longer the reluctant servants of the crown, they had fought a revolution and now they and their comrades had become the matriarchs of the country they had fought and sacrificed so much for. (*Courtesy of Kilmainham Gaol Archives, 21PC-1B55-23*)

Select Bibliography

Bateson, Ray, *They Died by Pearse's Side* (Irish Graves Publications, Dublin, 2010)

Capuchin Annual, 1966–1970

Catholic Bulletin, 1916–1917

Caulfield, Max, *The Easter Rebellion* (Gill and Macmillan, Dublin, 1995)

Clare, Anne, *Unlikely Rebels: The Gifford Girls and the Fight for Irish Freedom* (Mercier Press, Cork, 2011)

Conlon, Lil, *Cumann na mBan and the Women of Ireland 1913–25* (Kilkenny People Ltd, Kilkenny, 1969)

Coogan, Tim Pat and Morrison, George, *The Irish Civil War* (Weidenfield and Nicholson, London, 1998)

Crowley, Brian, *Patrick Pearse: A Life in Pictures* (Mercier Press, Cork, 2013)

Crowley, Seán, *From Newce to Truce* (Cork, no date)

Dolan, Anne, *Commemorating the Irish Civil War: History & Memory, 1923–2000* (Cambridge University Press, Cambridge, 2006)

Fallon, Charlotte H., *Soul of Fire: A Biography of Mary MacSwiney* (Mercier Press, Cork, 1986)

Fitzgerald, Redmond, *Cry Blood, Cry Erin* (Vandal Publications, London, 1966)

Fox, R. M., *The History of the Irish Citizen Army* (James Duffy and Co. Ltd, Dublin, 1944)

— *Rebel Irishwomen* (Progress House, Dublin, 1967)

Foy, Michael and Barton, Brian, *The Easter Rising* (Sutton Publishing, UK, 1999)

Foy, Michael T., *Michael Collins and the Intelligence War* (Sutton Publishing, UK, 2006)

Gillis, Liz, *The Fall of Dublin* (Mercier Press, Cork, 2011)

— *Revolution in Dublin: A Photographic History 1913–23* (Mercier Press, Cork, 2013)

Griffith, Kenneth and O'Grady, Timothy E., *Curious Journey: An Oral History of Ireland's Unfinished Revolution* (Hutchinson and Co. Publishers, London, 1982)

Kiberd, Declan, *1916 Rebellion Handbook* (The Mourne River Press, Dublin, 1998)

Litton, Helen, *The Irish Civil War: An Illustrated History* (Wolfhound Press, Dublin, 1995)

— *Kathleen Clarke: Revolutionary Woman* (O'Brien Press, Dublin, 2008)

MacDonnell, Kathleen Keyes, *There is a Bridge at Bandon* (Mercier Press, Cork, 1972)

Macardle, Dorothy, *The Irish Republic* (Irish Press Ltd, Dublin, 1951)

MacEoin, Uinseann, *Survivors* (second edition, Argenta Publications, Dublin, 1987)

Matthews, Ann, *Renegades: Women in Irish Republican Politics 1900–1922* (Mercier Press, Cork, 2010)

— *Dissidents: Irish Republican Women 1923–1941* (Mercier Press, Cork, 2012)

— *The Irish Citizen Army* (Mercier Press, Cork, 2014)

McCoole, Sinead, *Guns and Chiffon* (Government Publications Stationary Office, Dublin, 1997)

— *No Ordinary Women* (O'Brien Press, Dublin, 2003)

Mulcahy, Ristéard, *Richard Mulcahy (1886–1971): A Family Memoir* (Aurelian Press, Dublin, 1999)

Murphy, Seán and Síle, *The Comeraghs 'Gunfire and Civil War': The Story of the Deise Brigade IRA 1914–24* (Comeragh Publications, Waterford, 2003)

National Graves Association, *The Last Post* (third edition, Elo Press, Dublin, 1985)

Néeson, Eoin, *The Civil War 1922–23* (Poolbeg Press, Dublin, 1995)

North Inner City Folklore Project, *The Forgotten Women 1916–1923: Honouring All Women in the Struggle for Irish Freedom* (Dublin, 2008)

O'Brien, Paul, *Blood on the Streets: 1916 and the Battle for Mount Street Bridge* (Mercier Press, Cork, 2008)

— *Crossfire: The Battle for the Four Courts 1916* (New Island Press, Dublin, 2012)

O'Connor, Diarmuid and Frank Connolly, *Sleep Soldier Sleep* (Meseab Publications, Kildare, 2011)

Ó Duigneáin, Proinnsíos, *Linda Kearns: A Revolutionary Irish Woman* (Drumlin Publications, Leitrim, 2002)

Ó Dúlaing, Donncha, *Voices of Ireland* (O'Brien Press, Dublin, 1984)

O'Dwyer, Martin (Bob), *Tipperary's Sons and Daughters 1916–1923* (Cashel Folk Village, Tipperary, 2001)

— *A Pictorial History of Tipperary 1916–23* (Cashel Folk Village, Tipperary, 2004)

O'Farrell, Mick, *A Walk Through Rebel Dublin* (Mercier Press, Cork, 1999)

Ó Ruairc, Pádraig Óg, *Revolution: A Photographic History of Revolutionary Ireland 1913–1923* (Mercier Press, Cork, 2011)

Ryan, Anne-Marie, *16 Dead Men: The Easter Rising Executions* (Mercier Press, Cork, 2014)

Ryan, Meda, *Michael Collins and the Women in his Life* (Mercier Press, Cork, 1996)

Skinnider, Margaret, *Doing My Bit For Ireland* (Century, New York, 1917)

Scott, Ciara, *Constance Gore Booth: Madame Countess de Markievicz* (Kilmainham Tales, Dublin, 2013)

Taillon, Ruth, *When History Was Made: The Women of 1916* (Beyond the Pale Publications, Belfast, 1996)

Ward, Margaret, *Unmanageable Revolutionaries: Women and Irish Nationalism* (Pluto Press, London, 1983)

— *In Their Own Voice* (Attic Press Ltd, Cork, 2001)

Woggan, Helga, *Silent Radical: Winifred Carney 1887–1943: A Reconstruction of her Biography* (Siptu, Dublin, 2000)

Younger, Calton, *Ireland's Civil War* (Fontana Books, London, 1970)

ACKNOWLEDGEMENTS

There are so many people to thank who helped make this book become a reality. Firstly my thanks to Mary Feehan, who suggested that I do the book, and all the staff at Mercier Press: Wendy, Sharon, Patrick, Sarah and Niamh, and to Bobby Francis, who proofread the manuscript. I would also like to thank the staff at the National Library of Ireland, in particular Glenn Dunne, Berni Metcalfe and Keith Murphy; Harriet Wheelock and Fergus Brady at the Royal College of Physicians; Síle Coleman and David Power of South County Dublin Libraries; Dan Breen and the staff at the Cork Public Museum; Brian Kirby of the Capuchin Archives; and Noreen Nugent and the staff at Waterford County Museum.

Special thanks to Niall Bergin, Kilmainham Gaol Museum and Archives, and to Brian Crowley at the Pearse Museum. Thanks also to my colleagues and friends in Kilmainham Gaol who have been so supportive of this project.

To the staff of Military Archives, I cannot thank you enough: Commandant Padraic Kennedy, Captain Stephen MacEoin, Private Adrian Short, Corporal Andy Lawlor, Lisa Dolan, Noelle Grothier, Hugh Beckett, Captain Claire Mortimer, Sergeant David Kelly, C QMS Tom Mitchell and Lieutenant Deirdre Carberry. You are always on hand to answer all my queries and I sincerely thank you for all your help.

During the writing of this book I was overwhelmed with the response I got from the relatives and friends of the women who were involved. You have welcomed me into your homes, you have shared your stories with me and most importantly you have introduced me to some truly exceptional women whom I never would have had the chance to know. I am truly grateful as without you this book would not or could not have been written. You have kept their memory alive and I am so very grateful to Elisabet Berney, Ristéard Mulcahy, Constance Corcoran, Miriam O'Keeffe, John Brennan, Phyllis Foynes, Phyllis Seale, John Fullerton, John Long, Donal Gilligan, Therese Gilligan, Eithne Brady, Iseult McCarthy, Bob Hughes, Maura Deegan Kavanagh, Ruairi, Éamonn and Dympna Boyce, Delia McDevitt, Doreen Cleary, Anne and Éire Garvey, Deirdre Dowling, Margaret Curtin, Sean Hales, Michael Curran, Jim Ryan, Jim Fleming, Molly Cunningham, Richard Callanan and the descendants of Margaret McGuinness, Maureen Dawson, Henry Fairbrother, Sean Collins, Mike Connolly, Pierce Cafferky, Josephine Clarke, Donal Doyle (Rashers), Victor Edmonds, Mairead de h'Oir, Esther Hyland, Honor Ó Brolchain, Terry Crosbie, Terry Fagan and the North Inner City Folklore group, Sé and Noel Fleming, Stephen Carey, Audrey and Bernadine Flanagan, Mark Humphrys of Dublin City University at humphrysfamilytree.com, Anne May, Aileen Murray, Dave Kilmartin, Jim and Pat Stephenson, Martina Kearns, Eamon Murphy, Terence Breen, Colm McGuinness, Anne Regan, Mark Moloney, Kevin and Maureen Murphy, Therese Carroll, Donal O'Flynn, Maeve O'Leary, Lorcan and Treasa Collins, Liam O'Meara, Michael O'Flanagan, Aengus Ó Snodaigh, Cormac Ó Comhraí, Adam O'Leary, members of the Breslin family, Siobhán and Nora Treacy, Deirdre Farrell, Meda Ryan, Mary McAuliffe, Dominic Price, Cara O'Neill, Derek Scanlon, Christopher McQuinn, Ray Bateson, members of Irish Volunteers and the National Graves Association, Victor Laing, Pat Brennan, Ed Penrose, Ernst McColl, David Ceannt, Gráinne Keeley, Tom French, Sean Andrews, Paddy Lalor, Veronica and Philip Daly, Marcella Byrne, Con Brady, Joe Craven, Patrick and Valerie Couglan, Kate and James Lowe, and Tim Horgan.

Thanks also to Peter McMahon, Martin O'Dwyer (Bob), Phil Fitzgerald, James Langton, Diarmuid O'Connor, Frank Lane, Patrick Mannix, Dr Shane Kenna, Kevin (son) Murphy, David O'Neill, Enda Fahy, Ruairi O'Donnell and Ciaran Barry – your support and encouragement have just been amazing. My thanks to Paul O'Brien and Las Fallon, two great historians who are always on hand for a chat. To Mícheál Ó Doibhilín, I don't know if I can find the words. You have been with me from the start with this book and I am indebted to you for all your help. You are truly a diamond in the rough and I am proud to call you my friend and I thank you from the bottom of my heart.

To my family and friends, you have all been such a great support to me with this book and I am so lucky that I have you in my life. John, Pat, Mikey, Phoebe, Gerry, Elizabeth Govan, Lydia, Jack, Aunt May and my extended family, Catherine Murphy, Derek Horan, Ben Carolan and Natasha Murphy, thank you. My sister Mimi, you are just the best big sister anyone could ever hope to have. Uncle Pat, you have always been there for me and you are the best uncle anyone could ever dream to have. And to my fiancé, James, as always you have encouraged, listened, and gone out of your way to make sure I stuck with the book – even when I felt I couldn't do it, you kept me going and I am truly grateful for your love and support.

Finally to my dad, Mick, everything I have achieved in my life is down to you. You were always there for me and I just want to say that I am so glad that the star you picked that night long ago was mine.

INDEX

W